Good Manufacturing Practices for Pharmaceuticals

A PLAN FOR TOTAL QUALITY CONTROL

DRUGS AND THE PHARMACEUTICAL SCIENCES

A Series of Textbooks and Monographs

Editor

James Swarbrick

Department of Pharmacy
University of Sydney
Sydney, N.S.W., Australia

Volume 1.   PHARMACOKINETICS, *Milo Gibaldi and Donald Perrier*

Volume 2.   GOOD MANUFACTURING PRACTICES FOR PHARMACEUTICALS: A PLAN FOR TOTAL QUALITY CONTROL, *Sidney H. Willig, Murray M. Tuckerman, and William S. Hitchings IV*

Other Volumes in Preparation

Good Manufacturing Practices for Pharmaceuticals

A PLAN FOR TOTAL QUALITY CONTROL

Sidney H. Willig
Faculty of Law and Pharmacy
Temple University
Philadelphia, Pennsylvania

Murray M. Tuckerman
Department of Pharmaceutical Chemistry
School of Pharmacy
Temple University
Philadelphia, Pennsylvania

William S. Hitchings IV
Department of Pharmaceutical Chemistry
School of Pharmacy
Temple University
Philadelphia, Pennsylvania

MARCEL DEKKER, INC. New York

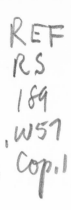
MARCEL DEKKER, INC.

270 Madison Avenue, New York, New York 10016

LIBRARY OF CONGRESS CATALOG CARD NUMBER: 75-23584

ISBN: 0-8247-6309-2

Current Printing (last digit):
10 9 8 7 6 5 4 3 2 1

PRINTED IN THE UNITED STATES OF AMERICA

Sci
R

CONTENTS

PREFACE

The purpose of the Good Manufacturing Practices regulations (21 CFR 133.1 et seq.) is to assure that all pharmaceutical products meet the requirements of the Federal Food, Drug, and Cosmetic Act as to safety and efficacy and have the identity and strength to meet the quality and purity characteristics which they purport to have, as required by section 501(a) (2) (b) of the Act. Nonconformity with GMP, therefore, establishes adulteration prohibited by section 301.

Reading part 133, one sees such phrases as "methods used," "facilities and controls used for," "to assure the quality and purity of," "that the equipment is," "key personnel involved," "components used in manufacture;" and subsections titled: "Buildings, Master Formula and Batch-Production Records, Productions and Control Procedures, Product Containers and Stability," etc. Basically, these headings circumscribe the topic of quality control. They are used by noted men in the field. They are regulated by law and they are, by their very nature, under the manufacturer's exclusive control. A manufacturer's responsibility for "control" is founded today in the law. When a manufacturer's plant, production, and control facilities and procedures do not conform to GMP, the act is violated, its purpose frustrated, and the consuming public's health jeopardized. The sword's other edge is a strong inference. Where an article marketed is adulterated or misbranded, can it not be inferred that some control procedure, whether in-process or not, is lacking or was bypassed? The axiom here preferred is: GMP is good quality control, is for the good of the public, is the purpose of the act, is good law, and is the manufacturer's responsibility.

One difficulty in Current Good Manufacturing Practices requirements, as interpreted by many, is that a finding of any degree of noncomplaince is equated with total failure. Since many deviations are retrospective in nature, that is, discovered after the product exists in finished form, the question arises of what is to be done to remedy the situation satisfactorily. Since Current Good Manufacturing Practices consist of standards which are consensually agreed to be both current and good, these techniques, procedures, and policies may combine the variances of superior as well as inferior techniques.

There is often, however, too much concern with what and how competitors making similar products are conducting similar operations. One doesn't have to know what a competitor is doing to be assured of compliance. One has to be satisfied that by the exertion of "appropriate" quality control methods only unadulterated and nonmisbranded products are being introduced into interstate commerce. The measure then is in the doing, in the results, rather than in the comparison with others. If the result is good and the job is being done correctly, there is every reason to believe, notwithstanding any combination of coincidences, that the quality and quantity of personnel, equipment, space, controls, and every other element of 21 CFR 133, are met. Despite increasing vigilance and conscientious anticipation of problems by administrators and scientists in industry and regulatory agencies, materials will be produced which are not safe and effective. As these problems occur and adequate testing and controls are devised, GMP regulations, of necessity, will change. The regulations, therefore, must be viewed as reflecting present knowledge, and must be expected to become more stringent and more explicit in the future.

The Food and Drug Administration has in the last decade evinced a will to be considerably more than an enforcement mechanism. It has done this, first, through the individual efforts of FDA officials, then through the Bureau for Education for Voluntary Compliance, and now by a composite effort of local and Washington officials and the Bureau of Voluntary Compliance. This latter unit, headed by General Delmore and his associates Fred Thornberry, Jonas Bassen, Don Early, and others, has done yeoman work in preparing the basis for effectuating the concepts set forth by Jonas Bassen in FDA Papers in 1968.

> First, that responsible firms will voluntarily correct conditions observed during establishment inspections which do not conform with Current GMP if they are adequately informed of the conditions.

> Second, that FDA and industry must be alert to recognize health hazards and promptly devise measures and practices to cope with them.

Third, that FDA has an interest in helping industry improve its quality controls to raise the quality assurance levels of its products. This means training industry personnel and instituting self-inspection programs (and the implementation or establishment of such a program by management is taken as a positive sign of GMP philosophy by FDA people).

Fourth, that FDA should provide individual firms interested in self-certification with training in inspectional techniques and technical expertise to qualify for the program and should continue with help and monitoring after they enter the program.

It is unfortunate for all concerned that there exist some disagreements between the regulators, the FDA, and the regulated, the affected industries, as to their respective rights and statutory duties.

Importantly, both are in agreement that consumer protection is in everyone's best interest; the FDA, because that is their mission and assignment; the industry, both as a matter of conscience and as a practical business outlook.

ACKNOWLEDGMENTS

The authors acknowledge with gratitude the patient and cheerful typing of the manuscript from frequently barely-legible copy and its multiple revisions by Catherine I. Cardamone, and the efforts of Byrde Merican Tuckerman and Abigail M. Tuckerman in preparing the index.

The proposed plan is not designed as a minimum- or regulatory-compliance program, but as an ideal plan to insure the quality of pharmaceutical preparations. It does have a sound economic base in that at every step the question was asked, "If this is not done, what are the probable economic consequences?" If the consequences are potentially more costly than the use of the indicated control, the control is recommended. Built into the system are such factors as quality control, security, personnel evaluation, and the inevitable trail of paper to show what was done, who did it and when.

The problem is approached from the point of view of a consultant with a free hand to suggest procedures. Recommendations are presented primarily as check lists covering aspects of quality control. Some areas of concern are indicated without recommendation of specific control procedures.

The Food and Drug Administration strives to insure that the regulated industries comply with a total quality control concept through its factory inspection programs, and through participation in voluntary compliance seminars and workshops sponsored jointly with the industries or with educational institutions. That a total quality assurance approach is necessary to prevent a drug product from being deemed adulterated under section 501 (a)(2)(B) and violative of section 301(b) of the Food , Drug, and Cosmetic Act is indicated by 21 CFR 133.1, et seq., Good Manufacturing Practice in the Manufacture, Processing, Packing, and Holding of Drugs. Nowhere in government documents, however, is there a comprehensive collection of specific measures to realize this concept. The concept of a total quality control system is not limited in scope to the analytical methods of assay, control charts, product inspections made during the manufacturing processes and prior to finished dosage form distribution nor to the statistical techniques utilized in these discrete operations, but also includes all control measures contributing to the completed market dosage form.

The Pharmaceutical Manufacturer's Association, in its *General Principles of Total Control of Quality in the Drug Industry,* published in June, 1967, states that "Total control of quality as it applies to the drug industry is the organized effort within an entire establishment to design, produce, maintain, and assure the specific quality in each unit of drug distributed. Total control of quality is a plant-wide activity and represents the aggregate responsibility of all segments of a company."

In the following chapters an attempt is made to provide specific guidelines and concepts which can serve as checks for critical operations within the entire organization so that a total quality control system may be achieved. Each requirement loosely generalized in Good Manufacturing Practice regulations is enlarged upon and made more specific to include measures which the authors believe necessary for good control.

The chapters are ordered by the subject matter of the sections of the Good Manufacturing Practices regulations.

Good Manufacturing Practices for Pharmaceuticals

A PLAN FOR TOTAL QUALITY CONTROL

Chapter 1

DEFINITIONS

21 CFR 133.1   Definitions.

(a) As used in this part [133], "act" means the
Federal Food, Drug, and Cosmetic Act, sections
201-902, 52 Stat. 1052 (21 U.S.C. 321-392),
with all amendments thereto.

(b) The definitions and interpretations contained
in section 201 of the [Federal Food, Drug, and
Cosmetic] act shall be applicable to such terms
when used in the regulations in this part [133].

The Kefauver Amendments of 1962 now classify drugs as adulterated unless
produced in conformity with part 133, Good Manufacturing Practices (GMP).

Almost all civil and criminal actions initiated by the FDA are derived
from violations of statutory definitions of misbranding and adulteration.
This is magnified both by the expanded areas of definition and prohibitions
created by the New Drug Amendments and by the prevalent judicial policy
of liberal construction of the statute with its prime objective of consumer
protection.

The adulteration statutes presently, aside from the regulations on Good
Manufacturing Practices, hold that the presence of a foreign substance even of
distinct and contrary appearance from the product itself, could cause it to be
adulterated. Previously distinct substances such as nails or pieces of a container not commingled in such a manner as to masquerade as a part of the food

itself, would not be considered an ingredient in support of a charge of adulteration. The courts have not, however, been entirely consistent as to this interpretation, and no doubt the subject regulations will be used to strengthen the FDA position of greater inclusion.

In 1952 a landmark decision in the 8th Circuit stated that a defendant might enjoy certain latitude where a "mere possibility" of contamination existed, subject to proof that factor conditions "would with reasonable possibility result in contamination." Obviously then, today's Good Manufacturing Practice regulations are viewed as the means for the FDA to present to the court this "reasonable possibility" based on breach of said regulations.

21 CFR 133.1(c), (d)

(c) As used in this part:

(1) The term "medicated feed" means any "complete feed," "feed additive supplement," or "feed additive concentrate," as defined in § 121.200 of this chapter, which feed contains one or more drugs as defined in section 201 (g) of the act. Medicated feeds are subject to §§ 133.100-110, inclusive.

(2) The term "medicated premix" means a substance that meets the definition in § 121.200 of this chapter for a "feed additive premix," except that it contains one or more drugs as defined in section 201 (g) of the act and is intended for manufacturing use in the production of a medicated feed. Medicated premixes are subject to §§ 133.200-133.210, inclusive.

(d) As used in §§ 133.2-133.15, inclusive:

(1) The term "component" means any ingredient intended for use in the manufacture of drugs in dosage form, including those that may not appear in the finished product.

(2) The term "batch" means a specific quantity of a drug that has uniform character and quality, within specified limits, and is produced according to a single manufacturing order during the same cycle of manufacture.

(3) The term "lot" means a batch or any portion of a batch of a drug or, in the case of a drug produced by a continuous process, an amount of drug produced in a unit of time or quantity in a manner that assures its uniformity, and in either case which is identified by a distinctive lot number and has uniform character and quality within specified limits.

(4) The terms "lot number" or "control number' mean any distinctive combination of letters or numbers, or both, from which the complete history of the manufacture, control, packaging, and distribution of a batch or lot of drug can be determined.

(5) The term "active ingredient" means any component which is intended to furnish pharmacological activity or other direct effect in the diagnosis, cure, mitigation, treatment, or prevention of disease, or to affect the structure or any function of the body of man or other animals. The term shall include those components which may undergo chemical change in the manufacture of the drug and be present in the finished drug product in a modified form intended to furnish the specified activity or effect.

(6) The term "inactive ingredient" means any component other than an "active ingredient" present in a drug.

(7) The term "materials approval unit" means any organizational element having the authority and responsibility to approve or reject components, in-process materials, packaging components, and final products.

(8) The term "strength" means:

(i) The concentration of the drug substance (for example, w/w, w/v, or unit dose/volume basis) and/or

(ii) The potency, that is, the therapeutic activity of the drug substance as indicated by appropriate laboratory tests or by adequately developed and controlled clinical data (expressed, for example, in terms of units by reference to a standard).

Chapter 2

FINISHED PHARMACEUTICALS

21 CFR 133.2   Finished pharmaceuticals; manufacturing practice.

(a) The criteria in §§ 133.3-133.13, inclusive, shall apply in determining whether the methods used in, or the facilities or controls used for, the manufacture, processing, packing, or holding of a drug conform to or are operated or administered in conformity with current good manufacturing practice to assure that a drug meets the requirements of the act as to safety, and has the identity and strength and meets the quality and purity characteristics which it purports or is represented to possess, as required by section 501 (a) (2) (B) of the act.

(b) The regulations in this part [133] permit the use of precision automatic, mechanical, or electronic equipment in the production and control of drugs when adequate inspection and checking procedures are used to assure proper performance.

Briefly, the section states that the company's adherence to the requirements of the entire 21 CFR 133 determines whether its output will be judged as adulterated or violative.

Adherence to the requirements initially necessitates an analysis of all current operations within the company which affect the quality of the finished marketed product. Such an analysis serves as a framework for structuring decision and information flows between managers, operators, technicians and other personnel who regulate product quality. An analysis of current conditions also divides the flow of materials into discrete, sequential operations, from the receipt and sampling of raw materials to final accountability computations during the market distribution, so that critical procedures may be specified and more closely examined.

The first step is evaluating the chances of establishing and maintaining a good quality control program. The first list, therefore, is a description of the management.

Management

1. Name of Company.
2. Address.
3. Telephone.
4. Number of years in business.
5. How is the company controlled? _____ independent _____ subsidiary.
   a. parent company
   b. address
6. Ownership: _____ corporation   _____ partnership
   _____ private   _____ other
7. Field of operation: _____ domestic   _____ foreign
8. Type of operation: _____ manufacturer   _____ repacker
   _____ packer   _____ other
9. Extent of operations.
   Plant Locations   *No. of Buildings*   *No. of Employees*
10. Current approvals: _____ FDA registration   _____ VA contract
    _____ Defense Personnel   _____ other
11. Membership in trade associations (showing professional interest).
    _____ Pharmaceutical Manufacturers Association (PMA).
    _____ The Proprietary Association
    _____ National Pharmaceutical Council
    _____ Parenteral Drug Association
    _____ Drug and Allied Products Guild
    _____ Other
12. Attendance at pharmaceutical meetings.
    Person   *Position*   *Meeting Attended/Date*
    Dissemination of proceedings to managers and supervisory personnel?

		Personnel	
Lecturer	*Subject*	*In attendance*	*Date*

13. To whom does it sell (approximate percentage of sales)?
    _____ wholesaler _____ hospital _____ physician _____ VA
    _____ direct pharmacy _____ Defense Personnel _____ other
14. How large is the sales force?
15. What consultant services are used (including outside laboratories)?
    Consultant:
    Training:
    Position when not consulting:
    Responsibility:
    Time per month:
16. In order for quality control to function properly, key executives must be approachable and sensitized by training or experience to quality control problems.

Title	*Name*	*Training*	*Experience*
President			
Vice-President			
Sales Manager			
Medical Director			
Plant Manager			
Production Manager			
Quality Control Director			
Laboratory Head			

17. Who has the authority to:
    a. reject defective material
    b. approve rework of salvageable material
    c. dispose of nonsalvageable material

It is important that quality control and production be kept separate and equal, usually by having the quality control manager and production manager report to the same executive, the plant manager.

It is prudent to permit personnel within both functions authority to temporarily sequester material considered to be defective or potentially deficient. The quality control function alone should have ultimate responsibility for removing a product at any stage in its processing into or from quarantine or into rejection status. Information from production should be utilized in arriving at the decision, but authority must be centralized and separated from the production function.

Define the functional organization structure, including in detail all functions that contribute to acceptance or rejection decision for a product or its components.

18. Packaging and labeling:
     In order to initiate quality control procedures, the dimensions of operations should be estimated. This requires the following information for the entire product line of the firm.

Type and Product Name	*Quantity Manufactured*	*Quantity Packaged*	
		own label	*other label*
Tablets			
Tablets, coated			
Tablets, multilayer			
Tablets, enteric coated			
Tablets, repeat dosage			
Tablets, sustained release			
Capsules			
Capsules, sustained release			
Liquids, external			
Liquids, oral			
Liquids, oral, sustained release			
Ophthalmic solutions			
Parenteral, sterile fill			
Parenteral, sterilized			
Syringe, prefilled			
Suppositories			
Granules, oral			
Powders			
Aerosols			
Aerosols, metered dose			
Sterile dressings			

How are the products promoted? (Obtain samples and package inserts)
_____ professional journal _____ lay journal _____ newspaper _____ other

The same procedures should be followed in assessing the operations of all outside contractors who contribute to the production of the finished pharmaceutical.

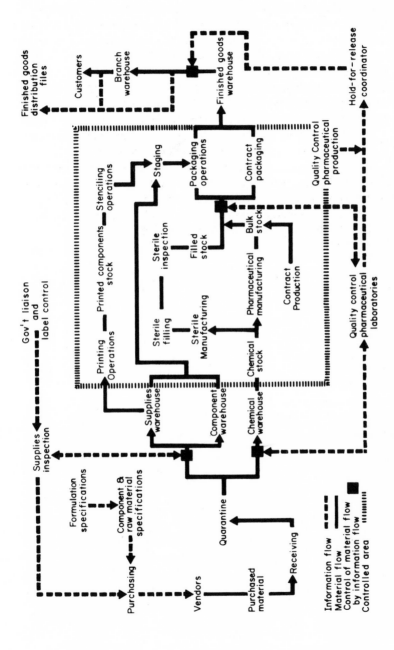

FIG. 1. Information and material flow with quality control surveillance.

Attention should be focused on the critical concepts of a quality control system. The production cycle for each drug must be controlled so that optimum quality levels may be attained for each manufacturing sequence. The efforts of all personnel making product integrity decisions during processing must be coordinated and standardized to attain these desired levels. The materials and accompanying information flow through production must demonstrate that management has determined potential sources of error and has introduced control procedures to minimize the possibility.

A model of material and information flows for operations show complete quality control surveillance of all operations involved with drug protection, adequate information exchange to monitor and control this surveillance, and records which document all activity. A flow chart depicting an analysis of current operations model with these considerations is given in Figure 1. More specific documentation and information requirements necessary to achieve control will be suggested in relevant GMP chapters.

Chapter 3

BUILDINGS

21 CFR 133.3   Buildings.

Buildings shall be maintained in a clean and orderly
manner and shall be of suitable size, construction,
and location to facilitate adequate cleaning, maintenance, and proper operations in the manufacturing, processing, packing, labeling, or holding of a
drug.

There are two major areas of concern, the external environment and the internal environment. Initially, the external environment must be amenable to
the location of well designed and constructed buildings. It is insufficient
that the buildings in which production operations are to occur are "clean
and orderly" and of "suitable size and construction." If the land, air, and
water resources which surround the plant create the possibility of water
damage, infestation, or contamination of any type, the facilities are in
jeopardy of being judged unsuitable.

Pertinent considerations prior to construction, purchase or alteration
of existing facilities include:

1. Insuring that the surrounding neighborhood is free from unsanitary environmental conditions:
   a. objectionable odors
   b. air, earth, and water pollutants

  c. filth
  d. sanitation hazards
  e. insects
  f. vermin
2. The premises are well drained with no flood threat existing.
3. Present and anticipated zoning restrictions are adequately stringent to prevent the above unsuitable conditions from occurring.
4. Water, waste removal, electricity, fuel, service, and utility deliveries are easily obtained—now and for future possible growth.
5. There is adequate transportation access and sufficient parking facilities.
6. The plant design permits security and controlled personnel access to research, production, and warehouse areas.

A basic concept is that the entire production site must be of adequate size, design, and construction to provide for controlled movement and storage of materials, as well as for contamination-free processing. All manufacturing, packaging, storage, and holding space must be maintained in a clean and orderly fashion to minimize the possibility of error.

21 CFR 133.3(a)

[The buildings shall:]
(a) Provide adequate space for:

(1) Orderly placement of equipment and materials [used in any of the following operations for which they are employed] to minimize any risk of mixups between different drugs, drug components, in-process materials, packaging materials, or labeling, and to minimize the possibility of [cross-] contamination.

(2) The receipt, storage, and withholding from use of components pending sampling, identification, and testing prior to release by the materials approval unit for manufacturing or packaging.

(3) The holding of rejected components prior to disposition to preclude the possibility of their use in manufacturing or packaging procedures for which they are unsuitable.

(4) The storage of components, containers, packaging materials, and labeling.

(5) Any manufacturing and processing operations performed.

(6) Any packaging or labeling operations.

(7) Storage of finished products.

(8) Control and production-laboratory operations.

The requirements of this section involve the actual design and construction of the plant site. The architecture must reduce to a minimum the likelihood of product, raw material, component, packaging, and labeling mixup or contamination. Considerations which affect the design of work areas are:

1. Adequate spaces to perform operations without crowding or disorder.
2. Physical barriers between some areas to prevent contamination and error.

Secondary considerations extend beyond available space to include the design of the building so that there will be control of material and personnel flows during processing operations. Neither operators, equipment, nor work-in-process should be moved through areas in which other operations are occurring. Hence the layout generally calls for rooms, cubicles, product lines, and areas to be segregated from common passages. In addition, a department which performs a single task such as mixing, encapsulating, or coating, and those which perform sequential operations such as granulating, compressing, and thin film coating, should be isolated with internal design considerations identical to those above.

It is also important that drug manufacturing procedures be kept apart from other nonrelated operations which occur at many large multifaceted pharmaceutical companies. This spatial isolation, when combined with controlled access policy, reduces the number of persons who might interfere with operations or serve as sources of contamination.

Table 1 defines the type of segregation which we believe to be necessary to adequately separate contributing operations. Those operations which require actual physical segregation (walls, partitions, or curtains), from all other procedures are keyed (1) in the table. Alternative methods of segregation are appropriate for other processes. These are indicated by the number following the procedure. An explanation of these items will be found in the notes after the table.

TABLE 1

Quality Control by Segregation of Operations

Function	Key
A. Receiving all input	1
B. Sampling all input	2
C. Quarantine of received materials	1, 3
D. Components storage	1, 3
E. Packaging materials storage	1
F. Label storage	1
G. Rejected components and materials storage	1
H. Weighing-measuring of components	1
I. Mixing	1, 4
J. Granulating	1, 4
K. Compounding and processing	1
Tableting	1
Compressing	5
Coating	5
Printing	5
Polishing	5
Inspection	5
Encapsulating	1
Ophthalmic clean area	1
Pre-filling storage	6
Penicillin products	1
Liquid manufacturing	1
Sterile products	1
Manufacturing	7
Components preparation	7
Filling	7
Visual inspection	7
L. Storage before quality release	7
M. Storage before packaging	1, 3
N. Filling and packaging	1
O. Finished goods quality inspection	1, 8
P. Finished product storage	1, 3, 8
Q. Shipping	1
R. Control laboratory	1
S. Animal quarters	1, 9
T. Equipment washing and cleaning	1, 10
U. Flammable storage areas	1, 11

Notes to Table 1

1. Physical segregation required.
2. The sampling of raw materials, components, and packaging materials could logically take place either at the receiving docks or after placement in the storage areas reserved for quarantined incoming items. Variables such as queue lengths, input quantities, sampling techniques, and the number of sampling personnel, will dictate the most efficient and effective placement of this operation.

All materials entering the manufacturing process must be sampled and inspected for conformance to preestablished acceptable quality limits (AQLs). Sampled material must be promptly and properly resealed to prevent contamination and marked by the person taking the sample. [See 21 CFR 133.6 (b).]

3. Those materials which require special storage conditions of humidity, light, and/or temperature control must be maintained in separate segregated areas which insure that these critical variables are controlled.

Good manufacturing practices require that there be minimum commingling of components, in-process materials, and finished products. Therefore, separate controlled environment areas must be placed throughout the materials flow network wherever periods of storage which would affect product stability are encountered. These include:

a. Raw materials receipt and quarantine.
b. Raw materials storage and issue.
c. In-process storage.
d. Finished bulk storage.
e. Packaged and labeled material storage pre-quality control release.
f. Finished goods warehouse.
g. Shipping cartons or vehicles.

The stability parameters specified for these items should include the time limits within which they may be kept under normal plant conditions without loss of potency. The containers for these materials should also have their special handling requirements prominently displayed on a label permanently attached at the time of receipt and when issued for production.

4. The degree of interdependence between two operations for any specific product might affect their degree of physical separation. If the two processes are sequential and continuous in nature, so that the same equipment is utilized for processing the entire lot in a closed system which

permits no additional material input, items (I) and (J) may be conducted in the same area. During the use of modular equipment, designated for processing a single lot of a given product the following procedures are mandatory:

a. The areas in which these operations occur are enclosed from floor to ceiling with a suitable material.
b. Each area is properly identified to include product name and number, lot and batch numbers being processed, assurance of equipment and room cleanliness and proper material being processed.

5. These in-process operations are normally performed with little time elapsing between each sequence. As a result, it is important not only to have adequate space in areas in which to perform the processes themselves, but also to have storage areas of sufficient size and location so there is no danger of mixing departmental material input with material output. The storage area must be outside the manufacturing cubicles to minimize opportunity for product mixup or contamination, and marked to indicate its storage function. This may be done in a variety of ways, including barriers, fencing, contrasting colors on walls and floors, so that the area is well defined. Each batch and lot number of production should be palletized or spaced so that there is no possibility of mixup between products or different lots of the same product. Identification by labels of both drums and drum lids in these areas is required.

The placement of equipment in these areas should conform to the following specifications:

a. Machines at least six feet apart (center-to-center) or eight feet apart if not in cubicles.
b. Tableting-encapsulating machines with hand-fed hoppers have partitions at least five feet high separating them.
c. Tableting-encapsulating machines with drum feeding mechanism (granulation in drum to feed drum to hopper) should have ceiling-to-floor partition between them.
d. Partitions should extend beyond machines so that bulk granulation and collecting drums are separated by them.
e. Each bay is properly identified for product, lot, and batch numbers being processed.

6. Opthalmic ointments and other semisolid preparations may be stored in the final manufacturing container during laboratory assay prior to filling and

packaging. These filled kettles must be covered completely and isolated at all times from any manufacturing operations to prevent the contents from being contaminated microbiologically or with particulate matter. A totally enclosed room with HEPA-filtered air, and controlled temperature and humidity is desirable for this storage space.

7. The design and arrangement of sterile operations spaces are being modified continuously as technological advancements in washing, filling, sterilization, and other associated operations are developed [1-3].

Basic requirements for the arrangement of sterile spaces are:

a. Aseptic areas are divided into segregated areas for the following functions and isolated from all other manufacturing operations.
  (1) gowning room with anteroom connecting it to filling and sealing room
  (2) cleaning room for containers and equipment
  (3) compounding room
  (4) filling and sealing room
  (5) gross particulate–leaker inspection room
b. Filling and sealing room are kept under positive air pressure in relation to other aseptic areas; all of the above spaces [(1) through (5)] in which containers, raw materials or other components of the finished product are processed at positive pressure to the surrounding nonsterile environment.
c. All accesses to sterile filling and sealing rooms have an anteroom. All entrances to anteroom closed with tight fitting doors so as to act as an airlock.
d. All aseptic-clean rooms are partially glass enclosed so that supervisors may observe operations without entering.
e. Outdoor facing walls are of solid construction with no windows.

8. Filling and packaging operations are completed most efficiently on an assembly line basis. The proper amount of approved bulk material is filled into the proper container, which is either prelabeled on the line or is being fed into labeling operations which are performed later in the packaging sequences. It is essential that these lines be constructed so there is no opportunity for either bulk material, packaging components or labels and labeling to commingle with other lines. These include:

a. A partition at least five feet high between the entire length of adjacent lines.

b. A line on the floor as means of demarcating packaging lines as limited personnel access areas.
c. Sufficient room at both ends of finishing lines to permit moving equipment to deposit and remove material without entering restricted areas.
d. Sufficient space within partitioned areas to permit storage of all material being utilized in any single packaging-finishing operation.

The inspection of finished products requirement may be accomplished on each finishing line providing that this operation is integrated into the system. Procedurally this requires that the person performing the inspection remain on the line and have no access to other packing operations.

9. Ideally, animal quarters would be located in a separate building removed from manufacturing operations. If not, they must be in a separate, enclosed room which is fitted with an anteroom to act as an air lock between the two areas and a separate air system.

10. Equipment washing rooms should be isolated so as to prevent water or moisture damage to products. An arrangement which provides both dirty and clean equipment ends to the cleaning operation is most satisfactory. The clean end could be adjacent to a clean equipment storage area to facilitate flow through the process and have access to the manufacturing areas in which the equipment is to be used.

11. Safety controls for flammable storage areas include:

a. Electrically conductive floor.
b. Raised door sill.
c. Blow-out wall.
e. Forced draft vapor take-off.
   (1) at floor level
   (2) near ceiling
f. "Rate-of-temperature-rise" firm alarm.
g. Fire alarm monitored at fire station or continuously-manned control board.
h. Switches for lights and vapor take-off fans located outside the room.
i. Supply of safety cans for dispensing fluids.
j. Alcohol storage located in this area meets Treasury regulations.
k. Heavy safe for storage of nitro compounds.

21 CFR 133.3(b)

[The buildings shall:]
(b) Provide adequate lighting, ventilation, and

screening and, when necessary for the intended production or control purposes, provide facilities for adequate air-pressure, microbiological, dust, humidity, and temperature controls to:

(1) Minimize contamination of products by extraneous adulterants, including cross-contamination of one product by dust or particles of ingredients arising from the manufacture, storage, or handling of another product.

(2) Minimize dissemination of micro-organisms from one area to another.

(3) Provide suitable storage conditions for drug components, in-process materials, and finished drugs in conformance with stability information as derived under § 133.13.

Subsection (b) requires that considerations, other than size and spatial arrangement, are required to be constructed into the building so that it may be in compliance with Good Manufacturing Practices. Thus the composition of walls and floors, the intensity of lighting, the method of air control and numerous other factors must be considered.

The following check points indicate areas requiring special attention of the quality assurance team:

Walls, Floors, and Ceilings

1. All are constructed of hard, nonporous, nonshedding material.
2. Material is able to withstand hot water and detergent cleaning operations.
3. Surfaces are free from any holes and cracks.
4. Surfaces of walls are flat, with recessed rather than projecting features.
5. All surfaces are free of peeling paint, missing tiles.

Permanent walls are best composed of a high-density block material, covered with a cementous material and smoothed and made nonporous by application of a high-density paint. Epoxy paints are extremely useful and durable for this function.

Floors of treated concrete, or floors covered with vinyl tile to eliminate dust formation during heavy use are recommended. Regular maintenance of these surfaces with cleaners, strippers, and coating agents is a necessity. All cleaning operations should be performed only when production operations in the area have ceased so as to prevent contamination.

Effects of residues on safety of personnel and on drug products must be determined for all cleaning materials prior to their use.

Suspended ceilings containing air diffusers and lighting fixtures maximize cleaning efficiency while reducing dust and particulate matter dispersion. The tiles used must be made of nonshedding material.

The air in all manufacturing and processing areas should contain minimal amounts of particulate matter, both viable and nonviable. This requirement may be met by a cooling and heating system that provides air entering these spaces in a nonturbulent flow pattern and in sufficient volume to remove airborne particles from locations where contamination of product may occur. Flow grates, vents, and vacuum dust removal equipment must be considered as part of the system design.

Ideally, an effective air conditioning, filtering, and humidification system will be employed in all new construction and renovations. For existing structures, where this is not feasible, GMP provisions require the use of screening with sufficient strength and gauge over all vents, grates, windows, and other openings to prevent insect and rodent entrance. Insect attractant and electrocution devices (Insect-ocuter®) located near all entrances should be an integral part of this type of system as are vacuum and exhaust systems to insure adequate circulation. This type of system is not permissible for areas where parenterals, ointments, and ophthalmic preparations are produced or handled.

Any air conditioning system design should consider the following factors:

1. Means for preventing the entry of airborne contaminants into work area.
2. Enclosed or semiclosed systems, recirculating only particulate-free air from space to space.
3. Sufficient incoming volumes of air with exhaust to "sweep" particulate contaminants from the air in a working area.
4. A vacuum or special exhaust system in dusty manufacturing or handling rooms to prevent settling of contaminants.
5. Temperature and humidity controls to insure maximum comfort throughout all climatic conditions.
6. Pressure dampers and diffusers to insure constant velocity (nonturbulent) incoming air.
7. Independent control of incoming air into each departmental area so different needs may be met. Control should be maintained over temperature, humidity, and velocity.

8. Absolute HEPA filters located in the system immediately before entrance into the space to prevent passage of microbial and microscopic particulate matter.

Sterile manufacturing, filling, and handling spaces require special air processing. HEPA filter units with laminar air flow are minimal requirements in those areas where airborne contamination of product may occur. The manufacturer must make a cost-benefit decision as to the extent of this system. In special areas, modular laminar flow units to enclose those operations during which the drug dosage form is exposed to ambient air may be sufficient. Vertical, rather than horizontal, laminar flow reduces the problem of "downwind" flow of airborne particulate matter over working spaces. It has been reported that an air velocity of approximately 100 ft^3/min is necessary to achieve class-100 working conditions for large enclosed areas.

The efficiency of the air handling system must be continuously monitored to insure that desired filtration is being achieved. Airborne particle counters or plates placed at critical locations in the manufacturing cycle determine the amount of particles per unit time. Records of these periodic checks should be maintained so that abnormally high readings may be detected and appropriate remedial action taken.

Adequacy of lighting at working levels should be determined for each location within the plant. Normally, this value should lie between 60 and 75 footcandles to ensure worker comfort and the ability to perform tasks efficiently and effectively. As with air conditioning, periodic checks of these levels must be made at predetermined locations so that lights may be changed when necessary. Records of these checks should also be maintained in a central location. Consideration should be given to periodic replacement of light bulbs as a part of routine maintenance, as entailing less cost than repetitive measurements of light intensity.

In building design, provision must be made for drains, water, and steam supplies to meet the requirements of maintenance. Access from the outside, such as utility lines, doors, windows, and loading docks must be designed to minimize insect and rodent infestation.

21 CFR 133.3(c)

[The building shall:]
(c) Provide adequate locker facilities and hot and

cold water washing facilities, including soap or
detergent, air drier or single service towels, and
clean toilet facilities near working areas.

The legal requirements of Good Manufacturing Practices specify minimum
facilities for personnel. Adherence to a "zero defects" type program, management concern with employee morale, and extra measures to insure minimum probability of contamination suggest more.

1. Eating facilities well segregated from all production areas are mandatory.
   a. eating and drinking permitted only in separate eating facilities; smok-
      ing permitted only where an adequate disposal is provided, and apart
      from production areas.
   b. prominent signs indicating these rules posted at entrances to produc-
      tion areas
   c. enforcement procedures against violators taken by management
   d. permanent facilities for breaks and people bringing lunches required;
      ideally, cafeterias serving hot meals to reduce amount of food, a
      potential contamination source, brought into the plant
2. For production and materials processing areas:
   a. drinking, eating, smoking, tobacco chewing, and expectoration
      prohibited
   b. tissues and closed disposal containers readily available
3. Lavatories and lockers:
   a. adequate in number for the number of personnel employed
   b. conveniently located to all areas
   c. hot shower facilities are provided
   d. disinfectant soaps are utilized
   e. adequate ash and waste receptacles provided
   f. periodic cleaning of the area during each shift with logging of times
      and conditions mandatory
   g. complete cleaning with cleansing and disinfectant agents daily; follow-
      up inspection by supervisory personnel logged
   h. specific rest area provided for female employees
   i. eating and drinking not permitted; foods and beverages for meals and
      breaks stored only in lockers
   j. lavatory and locker areas separated from all sterile spaces by an air
      lock
4. Clothing:
   a. sufficient amount of clean uniforms provided by company to personnel

b. regulations stipulating maximum intervals between changes for each function
c. workers in special clean areas wearing only lint- and dust-free garments to prevent shedding
d. where necessary the following articles are provided by the company:
   (1) hats and head covers for clean areas
   (2) aprons
   (3) safety shoes
   (4) gloves, disposable in clean areas
   (5) safety glasses
   (6) masks
   (7) protective goggles
   (8) disposable boots for clean areas
   (9) lint-free coveralls for clean areas

The following sections are either self-explanatory or have been previously commented upon in this chapter.

21 CFR 133.3(d), (e), (f)

[The building shall:]
(d) Provide an adequate supply of potable water (PHS standards in 42 CFR Part 73) under continuous positive pressure in a plumbing system free of defects that could cause or contribute to contamination of any drug. Drains shall be of adequate size and, where connected directly to a sewer, shall be equipped with traps to prevent back-siphonage.

(e) Provide suitable housing and space for the care of all laboratory animals.

(f) Provide for safe and sanitary disposal of sewage, trash, and other refuse within and from the buildings and immediate premises.

Further comment on section 133.3(f) will be found in Chapter 11, Laboratory Controls.

NOTES

1. T. Fornalsaro, "Design and Operation of a New Sterile Manufacturing Facility," *Bull. Parenteral Drug Assn.,* **24**, 110, 1970.

2. K. Goddard, "Designing a Parenteral Manufacturing Facility, *Bull. Parenteral Drug Assn.,* **23**, 69, 1969.

3. H. Loughhead, "Parenteral Production under Vertical Laminar Flow," *Bull. Parenteral Drug Assn.,* **23**, 17, 1969.

Chapter 4

EQUIPMENT

21 CFR 133.4   Equipment.

Equipment used for the manufacture, processing, packaging, labeling, holding, testing, or control of drugs shall be maintained in a clean and orderly manner and shall be of suitable design, size, construction, and location to facilitate cleaning, maintenance and operation for its intended purpose.

An extensive variety of equipment, manual, semiautomated and self-controlled, with automatically controlled feedback responses, is available today to the pharmaceutical industry. The evolution of this modern equipment is the answer to the rising costs and frequent inefficiency of manual methods, and has been accelerated by technological developments both from within the industry and from related external organizations. The requirement that pharmaceutical products meet optimum standards of purity, identity, quality, and potency, however, imposes limitations on the prudent manufacturer and requires that each piece of equipment purchased meet criteria more important than improved cost/efficiency ratios.

Equipment, like the buildings which house it, must be designed, constructed, located, and maintained so that the quality designed into each drug may be assured and repeated on a batch to batch production basis. Equipment and production methods must be tailored to fit the capability, capacity, and requirements of each other. Thus, testing and evaluating equipment effects on different dosage form standards becomes a strict requirement prior to purchase or design modification.

Following the determination of the dosage form for a new drug substance or the decision to purchase new or modify existing equipment, production engineering must assist in determining optimum equipment necessary for batch size manufacturing. Companies without this engineering capacity may have to rely on correspondence and specifications supplied by dealers and technical representatives.

Before any new equipment may be utilized for the production of drugs to be distributed through marketing channels, machinery-product profiles must be developed. This can only be done after a sufficient number of production size lots have been processed, numerous samples taken from each batch, and relevant chemical, physical, and pharmaceutical parameters measured. Enough samples must be taken so that the manufacturer may place high confidence that product variability does not exceed official or claimed levels. The sample size is then a function of the drug, its potency and degradation characteristics, as well as the characteristics of the machine.

Records of all acceptance and processing tests performed and results should be maintained in a central equipment log. Each piece of equipment should have a separate entry and include:

1. Manufacturer, model, serial number.
2. Purchased from, date, cost.
3. Size and output quantity.
4. Location in plant.
5. Maintenance responsibility and schedule.
6. Modifications made after purchase.
7. Tests performed (preacceptance and continuing performance).

All information pertinent to its use should be kept together along with later communications from the manufacturer, inspection, repair, and overhaul records, in such a way as to be available to production, engineering, quality control, and research and development.

Where the plant undertakes a certain kind of operation, specialized equipment may be in order. This might then require special care in overseeing, and, perhaps, personnel with special training. For example, a plant that has a substantial part of its output in sterile products, whether these be injectables or ophthalmics, requires special equipment locations, and a constant routing of maintenance to minimize hazards of bacterial contamination or other pathogenic seeding, as well as equipment and procedures to meet the need for freedom from pyrogens and particulate matter.

21 CFR 133.4(a)

[Equipment shall:]
(a) Be so constructed that all surfaces that come into contact with a drug product shall not be reactive, additive, or absorptive so as to alter the safety, identity, strength, quality, or purity of the drug or its components beyond the official or other established requirements.

To insure compliance with this subsection requires that the manufacturer determine accurately which drug products and materials are being processed in his plant, and where contact between machinery and materials occurs. Each of these points of contact must then be assessed to insure that no surface or mechanical part of the equipment in contact will add to, absorb, or react with the material, either as it exists in its pure form or in a manufactured state.

Since such a great diversity of equipment does exist, its selection depends primarily on meeting the specific requirement of the manufacturer.

Factors which must be considered include:

1. Aqueous and organic liquids normally are more reactive than solid dosage forms and might require special equipment for processing, e.g., glass-lined vats.
2. Reaction rates are a function of temperature. High temperature operations increase the probability of significantly affecting the purported purity, identity, or strength.

21 CFR 133.4(b)

[Equipment shall;]
(b) Be so constructed that any substances required for the operation of the equipment, such as lubricants or coolants, do not contact drug products so as to alter the safety, identity, strength, quality, or purity of the drug or its components beyond the official or other established requirements.

This requirement affects the design, construction, and placement of manufacturing equipment. Motors, drive belts, gears, and other sources of lubricant contamination must be located away from openings or surfaces where they might come in contact with the product. In high-speed tableting or encapsulating this requirement is difficult to achieve. Greater care, consequently, must be extended to keep Zirc fittings and lubrication tips free from extraneous matter which might fall into the product or interfere with processing. It is also necessary to use lubricants which are nontoxic.

21 CFR 133.4(c)

[Equipment shall:]
(c) Be constructed and installed to facilitate adjustment, disassembly cleaning and maintenance to assure the reliability of control procedures, uniformity of production, and exclusion from the drugs of contaminants from previous and current manufacturing operations that might affect the safety, identity, strength, quality, or purity of the drug or its components beyond the official or other established requirements.

Although not specifically mentioned, proper cleaning and maintenance procedures require both proper construction and placement of the equipment. Quite obviously the controls must be located so that they are accessible to the operator and designed so that they are intelligible to personnel with less than an engineer's training. Proper adjustments may be made only when indicators and effectors are operating properly, hence total machinery maintenance is required.

Most machinery has a factory-designed "preventative maintenance program" which requires that certain checks, adjustments, replacements, and maintenance be performed at designated intervals. Guarantees and warranties are contingent upon successful completion and proper documentation of these programs. Good Manufacturing Practice requires this and more. Equipment must be sufficiently disassembled to insure that a complete cleaning may take place between different drug products to insure that no cross-contamination occurs. Although it is permissible to process consecutive lots of the same product on the same machine without completely taking equipment apart for cleaning (exceptions: sterile products, liquids, semisolids, penicillins, narcotics), batch-to-batch integrity must be maintained for accountability. A time limit must be established for this practice. Normally, twice a week for complete cleaning procedures should be considered minimal, since excessive operation without complete maintenance increases the probability for nonuniform production and excessive variability.

Ideally, equipment should be portable so that it may be removed to special cleaning and maintenance areas. If this is not possible, its location must be amenable to complete cleaning procedures which also includes the presence of appropriate cleaning materials and provision for removal of wastes. Nonportable equipment must be attached securely for safety, preferably away from walls, ceilings and floors so that all parts are easily accessible for disassembling and cleaning.

It is important to remember that dusting with brushes may easily cross-contaminate a product and vacuuming can remove only gross particles not adhering to equipment surfaces. Certain cleaning solvents leave residues which become contaminants. Complete cleaning can be achieved only by disassembling the machine totally and using carefully chosen cleaning agents and procedures.

A partial check-list for the cleaning of vessels and pumps is given below.

1. Vessels.
   a. water under pressure is available
   b. steam is available
   c. all vessels are cleaned immediately after use
   d. clean vessels are labelled and certified by signature and date
   e. clean vessels are stored in a covered condition in separate designated space
2. Pumps.
   a. all pumps used in product lines are cleanable (centrifugal pumps are normally used and can be cleaned by removing the face plate)
   b. all product handling lines can be readily disassembled for cleaning
   c. a record of cleaning of pumps and lines is maintained
   d. the record is certified by signature and date

Good Manufacturing Practice requires that a record of cleanliness for each piece of equipment utilized during pharmaceutical production be maintained. A batch equipment record should be prepared for each piece of equipment in a department with the following data fields:

1. Department.
2. Machine name and number.
3. Specific step by step cleaning procedure.
4. Product and batch last processed.
5. Product and batch to be processed.
6. Operator and supervisor signatures—date.

After use of the piece of equipment and prior to cleaning, a copy of this form is issued. Following the specified cleaning procedure, a supervisor inspects and signs the record before the equipment is placed in the clean equipment storage area.

Prior to its use in the next batch, the equipment is rechecked for cleanliness and labeling. The record is then signed and dated by both the supervisor and operator and becomes a part of the permanent batch record accompanying the materials through production.

21 CFR 133.4(d)

[Equipment shall:]
(d) Be of suitable type, size and accuracy for any
testing, measuring, mixing, weighing, or other
processing or storage operations.

The capacity of any production machine cannot be exceeded if the machine is to survive and if the output is to be of desired quality. Thus the production quantity for any sequence in the manufacturing cycle becomes dependent on the capability of associated equipment as well as materials control, and the intrinsic physical and chemical properties of the ingredients. All these parameters must be statistically evaluated prior to equipment purchase, formula development, and implementation of production operations, so that production batches can be expected to possess characteristics identical with research and mock-up batches.

Balances and scales must reflect the purposes for which they are intended. It would be poor quality control to weigh out for production 500 grams of a potent drug raw material on a balance which can be read precisely only at 10-gram intervals. These instruments must be supplied in sufficient quantity so that each operation has a measuring device of sufficient accuracy and precision.

A program of routine maintenance and calibration for each of these instruments is necessary. Each should be balanced and "zeroed" before a weighment or measurement is taken. Standard weights and measures must be readily available so that operators may insure accuracy. Repair, calibration, and standardization should be attempted only by trained and experienced technicians, hence they must be available any time they are required. The organization of these workers must be arranged so that there is a minimum of bureaucratic red tape cutting before one can be freed. The use of a floating on-duty technician is recommended to insure optimum results.

As a final precaution, the balances and scales should be checked by an outside servicing organization (usually supplied through the manufacturer) on a stated periodic basis. Frequency of servicing is determined by the type of equipment and the extent of its use. For example, sensitive torsion balances may require servicing on a monthly basis, whereas beam balances may be serviced at half-yearly or even yearly intervals. Equipment logs, as previously described, should show a record of this periodic check.

Chapter 5

PERSONNEL

21 CFR 133.5   Personnel.

(a) The personnel responsible for directing the
manufacture and control of the drug shall be adequate in number and background of education,
training, and experience, or combination thereof,
to assure that the drug has the safety, identity,
strength, quality, and purity that it purports to
possess. All personnel shall have capabilities
commensurate with their assigned functions, a
thorough understanding of the manufacturing
or control operations they perform, the necessary
training or experience, and adequate information
concerning the reason for application of pertinent
provisions of this part to their respective functions.

The pharmaceutical output of any firm reflects the competence, interest, and
ability of its employees. Studies have estimated that about one-quarter of
all in-plant errors, responsible for defective material, are attributable to
personnel factors. These include disinterest, inability to perform an assigned
task, fatigue, and even intentional sabotage.

For the employer who desires to market drugs of consistently high
quality, it is mandatory to have employees who understand their assigned
tasks and are motivated to perform to the best of their ability.

Personnel assigned to each of the operations involved in the processing of nonfinished materials, manufacturing, packaging, and control of drug products must possess sufficient knowledge and proficiency to competently perform assigned tasks.

1. Scientific personnel must be qualified through recognized academic studies.
2. Technician's duties are not the same as those of the professional scientist.
3. Production workers may qualify without benefit of an academic degree if training and experience in the field are sufficient to insure competency.
4. Different levels of management require different proportions and total amounts of academic education, training, and experience.
5. Depending on the assignment then, through a proportionate combination of education and experience, each person must have demonstrated competency for the responsibilities of that assignment.

Several aspects of personnel control are important.

Who is Hired?

The evolving statutes of equal job opportunity presently dictate that the pharmaceutical manufacturer cannot discriminate against age, race, color, creed, sex, or national origins. Good manufacturing practices imply that the worker must be able to read with sufficient ability to understand written directions. Many companies have the in-house requirement of successful completion of a high school education or an equivalency test. Presumably the worker, no matter the entrance level, will advance to more satisfying and demanding jobs during his employment necessitating, ultimately, basic learned skills.

For management, scientific and technical personnel, hiring practices must be based on sound, comparable employment practices and also insure that the person and the position criteria are mutually suitable. Organization requirements must be met by the training and experience of the candidate.

Personnel Practices

One of the fundamental tenets of personnel management is that the organization must satisfy a set of basic, intrinsic, personnel hierarchial requirements before worker satisfaction may be maximized. A positive correlation between job satisfaction, productivity, and the desire of the worker to perform assigned tasks as required has also been demonstrated. It is beyond the scope of this chapter to describe practices such as vertical integration and job enlargement, which have been proposed as means of achieving greater worker satisfaction. It should be apparent that managerial expectations can be met only when worker expectations and needs are satisfied so that full performance skills may be realized. Suggested readings [1-3] on this topic are listed at the end of this chapter.

All personnel must be trained and indoctrinated in the performance of the tasks to which they are assigned. A period of formal training, including detailed procedures and quality requirements of the job is mandatory and must be commensurate with the complexity of the task to insure worker familiarity at its conclusion.

An inspector's report, described in FDA papers, noted an instance where: "In one case a firm manufactured a vitamin product which was contaminated with a sex hormone. Employees in the granulating room were pressed for more and more production. They found that they could save time if they ran all the granulations of one color through the Fitz mill without cleaning. They cleaned the Fitz mill only when the color of a granulation was different from the one previously run."

The cause of this error was lack of knowledge of the production operation objectives and inadequate training and supervision. What would such adequate measures have amounted to? Only the amount of training and supervision that would be reasonable to expect on the basis of average prudent manufacturing practices by this manufacturer's peers. What is reasonable? A maximum effort at training and communication with employees who have minimal educational and experience background as is necessary for carrying out the assigned task.

Postgraduate education for management, scientific, and technical personnel should be encouraged. Funds for investment in tuition repayment plans should be made available. Symposia, seminars, and conferences, in-house as well as external, should be used to provide education and training in appropriate areas. Circulation of journals and trade publications to concerned personnel helps maintain expertise.

Educational records must be maintained and kept current for all technicians, scientists, and management. Data fields included:

1. All periods of formal education and training, including company and industrial seminars.

2. Institution–dates–degrees.
3. Course titles–performance.
4. Special qualifications–proficiency with equipment–assays, etc.
5. Academic or industrial awards.

These records should be maintained in a central location with limited access. They should be considered a part of an employee's confidential file. Annual review by the personnel department with the employee indicates interest and concern with individual performance and position within the company.

Employees must also be rewarded for extraordinary achievement, contribution, or participation, whether this be in the form of remuneration or recognition. It must also be publicized that advancement is both available and desirable, for this serves as a source of motivation.

Employees should also be an integral part of any functioning total quality program. The personnel portion of quality assurance consists of:

1. Establishing production, quality, raw materials, and laboratory controls to include job descriptions, job responsibilities, facilities descriptions and operating instructions.
2. Provisions for communicating proper processes and procedures from immediate hierarchial supervisors to those employees directly affected.
3. Insuring adequate quantity and quality of supervision so that the job may be performed correctly the first time.
4. Means for encouraging communication at periodic intervals between and within job levels.
5. An employee error elimination program, "Zero Defects," "Q. S.," "Pride in Quality," etc., encourages everyone in the company to report to a designated manager any potential source of error and, if possible, corrective measures. These programs reduce employee and management error by inducing cooperation and a feeling of contribution between workers and management. They, however, are not fully successful unless well designed. They are not a substitute for standard operating procedures covering all aspects of production, an effective horizontal and vertical communications system, sufficient numbers of motivated, knowledgeable, and responsible supervisors and employees, and adequate facilities and equipment.

Safety Programs

Plant safety programs play an important role in quality control since hazardous conditions diminish employee moral and performance. This should consist of:

1. An active continuing safety campaign throughout the plant including:
    a. posters displayed prominently and changed often
    b. "days since last accident" sign continuously maintained
    c. safety bulletin boards listing recent plant accidents and methods of prevention
    d. safety inspection teams from several departments to audit work areas periodically
    e. lectures, movies
    f. safety equipment available free of cost to employees
    g. safety showers and eye baths in hazardous areas
2. All lines correctly and continually identified, including direction of flow:
    a. drinking—potable water
    b. water for injection
    c. gas
    d. vacuum
    e. waste
    f. work in process
    g. steam
    h. electrical
    i. communication
3. Fire extinguishers for all types of fires in each department or area. Locations conspicuously marked.
4. In-plant alarms available and locations marked.
5. Telephones available.
6. Fire exits conspicuously marked and logically placed.
7. Emergency lights and generators available.
8. Emergency fire drills held regularly.
9. Emergency teams including fire and first aid, trained and readily available during all working hours.

Special Aspects in Quality Control

Since the language that equates GMP failure with adulteration in the statute notes the need for operative and administrative conformity, it envisions responsible leadership by higher management personnel (the principal, the master) and adequate direction to employees (agents) to ensure proper "follow-through." Yet all levels of personnel must assume a good deal of personal responsibility for their own acts.

One compendium of advice on this subject [1967 PMA General

Principles of Total Control of Quality], has put it rather well: "Total control of quality is a plant-wide activity and represents the aggregate responsibility of all segments of a company. The responsibility for auditing the control system and for evaluating product quality is that of a specific group, 'Quality Control.' ... [The quality control supervisor] should be responsible to a level of management which enables him to exercise independent judgment. His responsibilities and authority should be clearly defined by management."

To administer and operate in his areas of control reasonably, the quality control supervisor must be separated from any responsibility or authority in production. He should be on an equal, but opposite, plateau of authority. Some feel the situation is most wholesome when the gap between production and quality control direction is evidenced by genuine unfriendliness. After all, in simple form, the production people are trying to produce the most goods in the least time and space with the smallest budget. Quality control is to certify that any goods produced under any conditions are of good quality from the legal and scientific view and analysis.

The quality control supervisor must have a questioning nature. Some say he must be naturally distrustful. This applies to all matters in his area, including calculations and conclusions reached by his peers and superiors from an organizational viewpoint. It certainly applies to findings submitted by vendors and vendees of the operation and by its subcontractors. If he's other than such, he will have to be a buck-passer.

In one incident that necessitated recall of all physician's samples sent out with a particular lot number, the batch record for the lot showed the quality control supervisor the likelihood that a possible error in the active ingredient percentage had occurred in the compounding, if the batch sheet had been followed for that active ingredient. Unfortunately, this review occurred after the samples had been released from quarantine for shipment to company salesmen. They had been held pending satisfactory assay receipt from an outside laboratory. The assay as received was similar in detail to previous assays for this elixir carried out by the same laboratory.

On notice from the quality control supervisor to reassay, they confirmed his suspicion that a transposed decimal point had resulted in the active ingredient being present in only 10% of the required quantity.

Advice given by the FDA on being notified that a voluntary recall was being carried out urged:

1. Better evaluation of the outside laboratory they were depending on.
2. Greater care in listing batch sheet information so that uniform systems of measurement are utilized.

3. Listings showing a zero before a precedent decimal point to help eliminate errors in reading and writing.
4. Leaving adequate space on batch sheets between listings that have a dangerous basis for encouraging error by similarity.
5. Checking batch sheets more capably and routinely for errors in formulation.

21 CFR 133.5(b)

(b) Any person shown at any time (either by medical examination or supervisory observation) to have an apparent illness or open lesions that may adversely affect the safety or quality of drugs shall be excluded from direct contact with drug products until the condition is corrected. All employees shall be instructed to report to supervisory personnel any conditions that may have such an adverse affect on drug products.

Personnel control measures include:

1. Preemployment medical examination for all employees including:
   a. chest X-ray
   b. Wasserman test
   c. Tuberculosis test
2. Periodic reexaminations, at least annually.
3. Maintenance of sick-leave records.
4. Requirement of a "fitness" statement from a physician, either company or personal, for return to work after sick leave greater than one week.
5. Maintenance of medical examination records and annual review of medical history.

There should be a liberal policy for those who feel fit for work but show symptoms of the common cold or other nondisabling illness. Employees will be reluctant to report these conditions if they are punished by being sent home, have their pay reduced, or are told to continue work since "it doesn't really matter." Ideally, these employees should be allowed to work in tasks in which they cannot contaminate products and at their usual rate of pay.

Separating a worker who is ill or one with open lesions from the product by use of gloves, masks, or special clothing is not recommended. The discomfort involved in their use tempts the worker to discard them when he is not being observed. The employee reporting requirement of this section will not be effective unless a set of specific conditions to be reported is provided.

Although not pertinent to the Act, one aspect of personnel health would seem to be the responsibility of the employer. When an employee is in contact with materials known to be physiologically active in small quantities, such as steroids, diethystilbestrol, antitumor alkylating agents, appropriate medical examination and clinical testing of body fluids should be performed at reasonably short intervals so that measures may be taken to prevent acute or chronic toxic effects.

SUGGESTED READING

1. J. Litterer, *Organizations: Structure and Behavior,* Wiley, New York, 1968.

2. E. Murray, *Motivation and Emotion,* Prentice-Hall, Englewood Cliffs, N. J., 1967.

3. E. Schein, *Organizational Psychology,* Prentice-Hall, Englewood Cliffs, N. J., 1965.

4. F. Delmore, "Industry Associations and Self Regulation," *Food, Drug, Cosmetic Law J.,* **24** 11, 557-564, 1969.

5. J. Saengen, "The Key to Quality Programs," *Bull. Parenteral Drug Assn.,* **23**, 179-185, 1969.
   [An excellent description of one company's quality assurance program.]

Chapter 6

COMPONENTS

21 CFR 133.6   Components.

All components and other materials used in the manufacture, processing, and packaging of drug products, and materials necessary for building and equipment maintenance, upon receipt shall be stored and handled in a safe, sanitary, and orderly manner. Adequate measures shall be taken to prevent mixups and cross-contamination affecting drugs and drug products. Components shall be withheld from use until they have been identified, sampled, and tested for conformance with established specifications and are released by a materials approval unit. Control of components shall include the following.

(a) Each container or component shall be examined visually for damage or contamination prior to use, including examination for breakage of seals when indicated.

These paragraphs establish guidelines for the manufacturer's control of materials utilized in the production of the finished product or of raw materials which ultimately are formulated into the finished dose. Raw materials and components must be properly identified and controlled under appropriate conditions for the individual substance. In addition, records and information flows must properly document the measures utilized to achieve compliance.

The control of components begins prior to their receipt at the manufacturing site. Raw material and component selection is a cooperative function of research and development, which determines the most economic quality of materials that have been found capable of consistently producing acceptable product; of manufacturing, which may have special requirements of physical characteristics because of processing equipment; of purchasing, which should assemble information on suppliers, quality levels, and costs; and of quality control, which writes minimum specifications necessary to insure suitable quality. The aim is to obtain the highest quality materials at a price commensurate with quality requirements. This can often be accomplished through a knowledge of the various manufacturing methods for a component or product so that certain undesirable intermediates are completely eliminated, or arranging with a manufacturer to supply only the better material from his regular production run (at no increase in cost).

Control begins with the selection of the source, and a reliable alternative, and the submission of appropriate component and raw materials specifications. The following information should be considered in the selection process:

1. Does the vendor make this material? (Usually the basic producer can give better service than the vendor who buys to round-out a line.)
2. Is the supplier's batch number normally printed on each container?
3. Is the batch number for a single, uniform lot? (Some vendors "accommodate" a buyer by shipping all containers of material under one order number with the same batch number even though the material results from several production runs. The size of the vendor's usual run should be determined.)
4. Does the vendor have a strong quality control system?
5. What other products are made by the vendor? (Alerts to possibility of cross-contamination problems.)

The most effective method of determining the practices of suppliers is through an extensive pre-contract-award plant inspection. For raw materials used in large quantity, for pharmacologically active ingredients, and for labels, this inspection is an investment in reducing defective material input into the plant.

Raw Materials Specifications

The most important criterion in the selection of the supplier is his ability to deliver material which conforms to predetermined specifications. Initially, specifications should be as few and as lenient as possible. Experience will dictate the imposition of new, more rigid requirements. Initial specifications to the vendor should include:

1. Statement of material:
   a. chemical name
   b. degree of hydration or solvation
   c. crystal form
   d. stereoisomer form
2. Statement of intended use and suitability therefor.
3. Statement that all material assigned to a single control number be from a single production run.
4. Appearance.
5. Bulk density.
6. Particle size range (for solids).
7. Identification tests.
8. Potency (assay). This should be by official or standard assay when available.
9. Purity (tests and limits for specific impurities).
10. Sampling scheme to be used during production.
11. Packaging requirements:
    a. containers to be used are satisfactory for shipping
    b. containers to be used are satisfactory in shape and weight for in-plant handling
       (1) size
       (2) container material—grade, weight, color, lining
       (3) closure-sealing materials
12. Identification and labeling of component containers:
    a. name of product
    b. grade or quality
    c. name of supplier
    d. proper shipping address of purchaser
    e. supplier's lot or code number
    f. purchaser's identification number
13. A clause allowing revision of specifications as the purchaser deems appropriate.

14.   A guarantee that all materials will conform to the standards of the
      specifications.

Receiving

The receipt of ordered components and raw materials at the drug manufacturing site initiates a sequence of documentation and information flows that accompanies them through the entire production and distribution cycles. All
components used in manufacture and processing of drugs, regardless of
whether they appear in the finished product, are to be identified, stored, examined, tested, inventoried, handled, and otherwise controlled in a manner
to assure conformity to standards of identity, strength, quality, purity, and
freedom from contaminants that are consistent with their origin, storage, and
use. It is obvious that material which is not properly labeled or has been damaged in transit should not be accepted by the drug manufacturer.
      Visual examination at the receiving docks should include checks for:

1. Intact container, lids, and seals.
2. Evidence of water damage.
3. Evidence of rodent or insect infestation.
4. Proper labeling affixed in the specified manner.

      Containers not meeting the requirements of this examination are not ac-
cepted and should be returned to the vendor.
      If the material is accepted, receipt is recorded in a receiving log at the
point of entrance to the plant. This permanently-bound book, maintained by
the receiving function has the following data fields:

1. Date of receipt.
2. Control number assigned by receiving company.
3. Product identification—name and number used by receiving company.
4. Quantity contained in each control number. A control number should
   include only material from a single manufacturing cycle.
5. Supplier or vendor.
6. Stock or control number assigned by supplier.
7. Purchase order number.
8. Bill of lading number of shipper.

      Once the receipt is logged, the control number assigned to each compo-
nent lot by receiving must be conspicuously marked on each component

container so that all material utilized during production may be traced and controlled. In addition, all pertinent information should be transmitted to purchasing and the inventory control departments for their records and use. Purchasing must be notified when materials are refused entry so that an investigation may be initiated with the vendor.

The receiving supervisor must assign a separate control number to each incoming material with a different vendor's control or lot number in the sequence in which it received, unless a system is established in which raw materials are always identified by the number assigned to the original purchase requisition. This permits these materials to be more easily handled and used on a first in-first out basis. It is also desirable to maintain a separate sampling log indicating:

1. Name or initials of person sampling the component.
2. Final disposition following inspection.
3. Person taking control over material following disposition.
4. Dates for these operations.

The properly identified received material must be labeled conspicuously to show its quarantine status, then isolated and stored in a quarantine area to prevent its use in production prior to laboratory approval. Segregation presents difficulties at times, but none of these are insurmountable and physical separators can be innovated. In the end, this not only satisfies the FDA, but it makes for better organization and easier access and identification of the materials. It also simplifies rotation of stock and helps eliminate the potential waste that might come from aging and continued storage.

The storage area must provide the conditions necessary to maintain product physical or chemical integrity, including control of temperature, moisture, and humidity and other requirements when necessary. The requirement is also specific that the material itself must not become contaminated chemically, microbiologically or by vermin, dust, or other particles. Likewise, the material itself cannot serve as a source of contamination to other materials in the plant. This storage and handling requirement exists for all locations within the plant.

21 CFR 133.6(b), (c), (d), (e)

[Control of components shall include the following:]
(b) An adequate number of samples shall be taken
from a representative number of component

containers from each lot and shall be subjected to
one or more tests to establish the specific identity.

(c) Representative samples of components liable to
contamination with filth, insect infestation, or
other extraneous contaminants shall be appropriately examined.

(d) Representative samples of all components intended for use as active ingredients shall be tested
to determine their strength in order to assure conformance with appropriate specifications.

(e) Representative samples of components liable
to microbiological contamination shall be subjected to microbiological tests prior to use. Such
components shall not contain micro-organisms
that are objectionable in view of their intended
use.

Despite the fact that components and raw materials are normally received
from a reliable source, accompanied by an accurate protocol assay, and
are used shortly thereafter in the manufacturing cycle, all components must
be both qualitatively and quantitatively tested in order to insure the fitness
of the finished product.

Quality control laboratories must be notified of materials to be
sampled. This is normally accomplished by the receiving function transmit-
ting a receiving-sampling form to the laboratory.

Sampling Card

A sampling card form is prepared by the receiving department for each lot
of incoming material. The primary copy may be retained by receiving as a
permanent record of all materials input. A copy is forwarded to the
chemical and/or microbiological laboratory and acts as the primary materials
input identifier for laboratory records. This form lists:

1. Date.
2. Product name, number, grade.
3. Supplier and supplier's lot number.
4. In-house control number assigned.
5. In-house purchase order number.

6. Delivery method, shipper, numbers.
7. Quantity—number of containers and amount in each.

It may be sufficient for receiving to fill in and retain only the above items for internal records. The form, however, should contain additional data field for use by the analytical laboratories in their required records:

8. Statement of intended use.
9. Sample plan utilized for laboratory specimen.
   a. sample specification for quantity obtained
   b. type of container to be used for sample
   c. number of samples taken
   d. number of containers sampled
10. Appearance and condition of containers and affixed labels.
11. Sampler from laboratory signature.
12. Receiving department supervisor signature.
13. Quality control laboratory supervisory signature.

The requirement for "representative samples" to determine purity, identity, strength, and quality should extend to all materials utilized in pharmaceutical production, not just active ingredients. The possibility of chemical contamination and of microbiological and other impurities being present in excipients requires the prudent manufacturer to exercise greater precaution than prescribed. The representative sample is achieved by removing sufficient raw material from enough containers to obtain an idea of the composition of the entire lot. This should be based on the number of incoming containers per control number. Even though the contents assigned to each control number are presumed to be homogeneous, the sampling must be done from a number of containers and from a number of locations within the containers. Procedures include:

1. Draw random samples from a predetermined number of containers assigned to each control number.
2. Label samples with information present on container of components.
3. Reseal and replace sampled container. Mark container "sampled."
4. Verify sampling before and after drawing with receiving supervisor to complete the documentation.

Control procedures carried out by the laboratories for each component insure that the established specifications are in fact shown by received goods. For raw materials it includes verification of those items delineated under the product specifications, NDA, or other documents. Quality control, however, must not only be cognizant of in-house established specifications, but official requirements for each item.

Packaging and labeling components requirements will be presented in the sections for 21 CFR 133.9 and 10.

21 CFR 133.6(f), (g), (h)

[Control of components shall include the following:]
(f) Approved components shall be appropriately identified and retested as necessary to assure that they conform to appropriate specification of identity, strength, quality, and purity at time of use. This requires the following:

(1) Approved components shall be handled and stored to guard against contaminating or being contaminated by other drugs or components.

(2) Approved components shall be rotated in such a manner that the oldest stock is used first.

(3) Rejected components shall be identified and held to preclude their use in manufacturing or processing procedures for which they are unsuitable.

(g) Appropriate records shall be maintained, including the following:

(1) The identity and quantity of the component, the name of the supplier, the supplier's lot number, and the date of receipt.

(2) Examination and tests performed and rejected components and their disposition.

(3) An individual inventory and record for each component used in each batch of drug manufactured or processed.

(h) An appropriately identified reserve sample of all active ingredients consisting of at least twice the quantity necessary for all required tests, except those for sterility and determination of the presence of pyrogens, shall be retained for at least 2 years after distributions of the last drug lot incorporating the component has been completed or 1 year after the expiration date of this last drug lot, whichever is longer.

The results of the component analysis dictate future control measures. Rejected material which does not meet acceptable quality specifications must be:

1. Labeled or tagged to indicate status, including:
    a. product identification—name and number
    b. control number assigned
    c. quantity rejected
    d. rejection number or other suitable means of controlling reject material
2. Retained in isolation until returned to vendor or otherwise suitably disposed.

Notification must be made to:

1. Receiving—to relocate material.
2. Purchasing—stock status inventory functions.

Material accepted for processing by the quality laboratory must be controlled so that its characteristics are not altered before the manufacturing processes. Appropriate measures include:

1. Notification to receiving—to remove the lot of raw material from the quarantine area.
2. Removal of "quarantine" label.
3. All containers tagged as "laboratory approved." Permanent label to include:
    a. product identification—name and number
    b. control number
    c. expiration date beyond which retesting is necessary
    d. date of release by laboratory
4. Containers removed to proper storage conditions for transfer into production cycle on a first in-first out basis.

Laboratory Records for Raw Materials

The quality control laboratory must maintain files which record the assays and tests performed on raw materials and components assigned to each issued control number. The records may be indexed either by the control numbers in consecutive order or by the identity of the material (item numbers). The files should also indicate the location of the retained sample.

The sampling card, which is transmitted by the receiving function, serves as the initial information input to the laboratories. A laboratory then establishes a separate file for each assigned component control number. This record lists all the procedures, tests, and assays performed which enable the laboratory to make an accept-reject recommendation.

Raw Materials Card

This document contains the following data fields:

1. Component–raw material name and identifying item number.
2. Control number assigned by receiving.
3. Purchase order number.
4. Supplier's lot number.
5. Quantity received and date of arrival.
6. All tests performed–including microbiological examination.
7. Applicable testing standards with cross reference to official, in-house, or raw materials specifications.
8. Results of tests performed.
9. Chemists or analysts performing tests.
10. Accept or reject recommendation.
11. Supervisory signature with date.

Acceptance Labels Control

The laboratory should also control the removal of approved components from quarantine before their use. The most satisfactory method is to require the control function to affix "release labels" to each container in the approved lot. Only one label for each container should be prepared–mimeograph or other duplicating methods are satisfactory for large lots–and these should be assigned to a specific employee for attachment. This should be recorded in a special log containing the following data items:

1. Component name and identification.
2. Control number assigned.
3. Number of containers in lot and labels received.
4. Signature of person taking custody.
5. Date.

The function of this procedure and the record is to reduce the probability of incorrect or nonapproved components entering the manufacturing cycles.

A similar record should be retained for rejected components. This record also contains information concerning the disposition of the unsatisfactory material.

Raw Material Issue

A specialized pharmaceutical or chemical component issuance section is the ideal method for maintaining control and releasing proper amounts of proper ingredients to the manufacturing process. Records maintained by this department itemize and inventory approved components and permit accountability of all raw materials issued for specific lots and batches.

Maximum control over all chemicals must be insured at this vital stage in production. These include:

1. Only materials which have been approved for use by the quality control laboratories permitted in area.
2. All containers of raw materials tagged to indicate laboratory release and showing date of expiration for use.
3. All containers being used as a source of raw materials for consecutive weighments labeled to show dispensing to each production lot or batch number with issued quantity.
4. Materials issued to assigned formula only after supervisory approval of proper amounts.
5. A system of "doers" and "checkers" utilized to verify amounts and identities of measured quantities.
6. Signatures recorded of all personnel handling or checking materials.

An order for the pharmacy function to issue raw materials is generally initiated by a production planning and control section. It is transmitted most effectively and with the lowest possibility of error by a copy of the master batch formula listing the proper ingredients and correct amounts for the lot or batch. Issuing records must show the specific amounts of designated ingredients entering production to enable tracing of raw materials through manufacturing and, ultimately, distribution cycles.

Component Record

This file lists by component name and item number, as well as the control number assigned at plant entry, the issuance of all components to the batch or lot of production. It must include the following data fields:

1. Component name and identification number.
2. Control number assigned at receiving.
3. Quantity received—number of containers and amount in each container.
4. Name and item number of each product in which the component was used.
5. Batch or lot number utilizing the component.
6. Amount used in each lot or batch.
7. Date used.
8. Inventory and accountability computations.
9. Supervisor or person making entry.

Each component assigned a different control number should have a file.

Container Records

Each container being utilized as a source of raw material for numerous lots or batches should be labeled to indicate this status. This tag could serve as a double check for reconciling the amounts required and actual amount taken from the container after each weighing. It should include:

1. Component name and identification number.
2. Control number.
3. Quantity in container (gross - tare = net weight).
4. Batch or lot number in which used.
5. Quantity issued to lot or batch number.
6. Weigher and checker's names and date of issue.

The tag is completed after each weighing is made and the quantity in the container checked against the theoretical balance. If the two do not coincide, an investigation must satisfactorily explain any discrepancy before the materials may be released.

Component Suppliers

The section on components affects not only the drug manufacturer, but also his suppliers and repackers of his product. With reference to foods specifically and hence to cosmetics and drugs by inference, "components" include materials which are never consumed without further processing. Since many components are purchased, it is instructive to examine the obligations of the manufacturer of the finished product and the obligations of the supplier.

For New Drug Applications, the manufacturer must supply a statement identifying each person who performs any part of the operations and designating his part, as well as a signed statement from each such person fully describing, directly or by reference, the methods, facilities, and controls of his part of the operation. A strict reading of the regulations, coupled with this requirement for the NDA, seems to require the manufacturer to obtain the same information from his contractors that he himself would be required to maintain if the operation were carried out in his own plant.

The doctrine of McPherson v. Buick, which is followed rather uniformly in the field of product liability, finds the manufacturer of the finished product liable to an injured litigant for faulty components. The sole remedy of the manufacturer who has processed the faulty material is in seeking an indemnity from the supplier.

In Wilson v. Faxen-Williams, in which the manufacturer only labeled the product, the case was decided for the plaintiff. The civil court held that the liability belonged to the party responsible for placing the product in commerce.

When a manufacturer of chemicals supplies a raw ingredient to a pharmaceutical manufacturer, it is necessary for the chemical manufacturer to abide by all the requirements of the regulations, if the chemical meets the definition of the drug in section 201(g) of the Act: "articles intended for use as a component" in "articles intended for use in the diagnosis, cure, mitigation, treatment, or prevention of disease in man or other animals."

Although it is specifically prohibited in 1.5(h), subsection of section 303(c) (3) of the Act, to represent or suggest that an article is guaranteed under the Act in its labeling, appropriate guaranties should be received with components, including assurance of proper registration with the Food and Drug Administration pursuant to section 510 of the Federal Food, Drug, and Cosmetic Act. This can be accomplished by a continuing guaranty as shown in Example A.

EXAMPLE A

Be advised that the undersigned has accomplished proper registration with the Federal Food and Drug Administration, pursuant to section 510 of the Federal Food, Drug, and Cosmetic Act dated _____ .
FURTHER,

The undersigned hereby guarantees that no food, drug, device, or cosmetic constituting, or being part of, any shipment or other delivery now or hereafter made to you by the undersigned will, at the time of such shipment or delivery, be adulterated or misbranded within the meaning of the Federal Food, Drug, and Cosmetic Act, or within the meaning of any applicable state or municipal law in which the definitions of adulteration and misbranding are substantially the same as those contained in the Federal Food, Drug, and Cosmetic Act as said Act and such laws are constituted and effective at the time of such shipment or delivery, or will be an article which may not, under the provisions of section 404 or 505 of said Act, be introduced into interstate commerce.

This guaranty shall be a continuing guaranty and shall be binding upon the undersigned with respect to all foods, drugs, devices and cosmetics shipped or delivered to you by the undersigned (including goods in transit), before the receipt by you of written notice of the revocation thereof.

Signed:

Company Name _____

Title _____

Address _____

Dated: _____

[Where appropriate, an additional guaranty may be incorporated:]

"A guaranty is also hereby given that no shipment or delivery now or hereafter made to you by the undersigned will, at the time of such shipment of delivery, be in violation of any of the provisions of the Federal Hazardous Substances Labeling Act."

If the purchase or shipment involves coal-tar colors and the manufacturer is domestic, the following guaranty should be obtained.

EXAMPLE B

AS PER SECTION 303(c) (3) OF THE FEDERAL FOOD, DRUG, AND COSMETIC ACT.

_____ hereby guarantees that all coal-tar colors listed herein were manufactured by him, and are from batches certified in accordance with the applicable regulations promulaged under the Federal Food, Drug, and Cosmetic Act.

Company Name _____

Signature _____

Title _____

Address _____

If the color is from a foreign manufacturer the guaranty should be as below (Example C), signed by such manufacturer and by his agent who resides in the United States.

EXAMPLE C

AS PER SECTION 303(c) (3) OF THE FEDERAL FOOD, DRUG, AND COSMETIC ACT.

_____ hereby severally guarantee that all coal-tar colors listed herein were manufactured by _____ , and are from batches certified in accordance with the applicable regulations promulgated under the Federal Food, Drug, and Cosmetic Act.

        Company Name _____

        Signature _____

        Title _____

        Address _____

Repackaging: Exemptions for Drugs and Devices—Section 503 of the Federal Food, Drug, and Cosmetic Act

The retail or dispensing container of food, drugs, and/or cosmetics, when shipped, or held after shipment, in interstate commerce, must comply with certain labeling and packaging requirements of the Federal Food, Drug, and Cosmetic Act. The FDA is directed to promulgate regulations that exempt drugs and devices from the labeling and packaging requirements set out in section 502 and its effectuating regulations.

These are restricted by section 503(a) to drugs and devices which are as a trade practice intended to be processed (undefined), labeled, or repacked.

1. In substantial quantities.
2. At establishments other than those where originally processed or packed.
3. Provided that such drugs and devices are not adulterated or misbranded, according to the criteria of the Act, when they leave this secondary processor, labeler or repacker's establishment.

To effectuate this legislative directive the FDA published the 1.107 regulations which have the effect of law.

Section 1.107(a) notes that the duration of such an exemption extends from the time of introduction into interstate commerce, time actually in interstate commerce (freight or shipment time), and the time it enters and is held in the secondary establishment so they may do the assigned work with it. Such time of exemption from the labeling and packaging requirements of section 501(b) which deals with compendial similarity and labeling, and of 502(b) (address, quantity, and count); 502(d) (habit-forming designation); 502(e) (nonproprietary name and setting out of ingredients); 502(f) directions, usage, warnings; 502(g) compendial requirements.

It is predicated on two alternative factors:

1. The primary shipper is actually the operator of the secondary establishment as well; e.g., the Pfizer plant at Terra Haute sends material to its Groton, Connecticut, plant for further processing, or,

2. If the primary operator is unrelated in ownership to the secondary operator, the shipment must be preceded by a written agreement signed by the parties and containing their business addresses. This is usually kept, in copy, in the "job jacket."

This agreement must spell out the specifications for processing, labeling, or repacking to insure that as followed the drug or device will as completed be nonviolative of the adulteration or misbranding provisions of the Act. While this can be incorporated in the regular contract between the parties, to do so risks exposure of the total contract to agency inquiry on the basis of their right to examine this writing for two years (both parties) after final shipment or delivery of such drug or device from the establishment.

Bear in mind, that there is no need, legally, nor should it be assumed, that the completed product must be returned to the primary party. Very often it may go immediately to third parties involved with distribution of the product—such as wholesalers, mailing houses, sales agents.

This requirement is one that is all too frequently forgotten with old drugs and devices, and with new drugs. With the latter there are additional requirements per section 505 and the 130 series of regulations.

Section 1.107(b)—subsequent removal from the secondary location of the same operator, of an adulterated or misbranded final product—makes the exemption void ab initio. And it is likewise violative [1.107(c)] if during the 2-year period the FDA is refused inspection of the *copy* of the agreement.

Section 1.107(d) ends any exemption gained under 1.107(a)(2) for similar reasons as 1.107(b) and (c).

Sections 1.107(e), (g), and (h) are somewhat the same as the foregoing for antibiotics, adding exemption from 502(1) which deals with need for batch certification and release.

It should be noted that the exemption is available for interstate shipments of bulk material to be repackaged at an establishment other than where the goods were originally processed provided that such shipment is covered under a written agreement between the one who ships the bulk and the one who repackages it. Records of the agreement (see Example D below) must be kept until two years after the final shipment or delivery of such drug from such an establishment. Copies of these records are to be available for inspection by the FDA. If no agreement is available, or on refusal to show the inspector a copy of such agreement, the exemption shall be declared void ab initio, and all material may be declared misbranded, with appropriate penalty.

EXAMPLE D

IN ACCORDANCE WITH PARAGRAPH 1.107 OF THE GENERAL REGULATIONS OF THE FOOD, DRUG, AND COSMETIC ACT.

The parties, supplier and customer, contemplate that this order, placed and acknowledged, signed by and containing the post office address of the supplier, shall constitute a written agreement within the meaning of paragraph 1.107 of the General Regulations, Federal Food, Drug, and Cosmetic Act; that it contains such specifications for the processing, labeling, repackaging, as the case may be, of such drug or device in such establishment as will insure, if specifications are followed, that such drug or device will not be adulterated or misbranded within the meaning of the Act upon completion of such processing, labeling, or repacking. It is further understood that this record of agreement will be kept until two years after the final shipment or delivery of such drug from such establishment. Exemption from compliance with the labeling and packaging requirements of sections 501(b) and 502(b), (d), (e), (f) and (g) is claimed thereon.

SEE ATTACHMENTS HERETO, PART OF THIS AGREEMENT:

_____ Company Name _____
_____ Signature _____
_____ Title _____
_____ Address _____

The repackager, to protect himself, may submit for his customer's signature an agreement somewhat similar in scope (Example E).

EXAMPLE E

<u>   *(date)*   </u>

The parties to this agreement, <u>   *(name)*   </u> ,
<u>   *(address)*   </u> , and <u>   *(name)*   </u> ,
<u>   *(address)*   </u> ;

Being cognizant of the service rendered to <u>   *(customer)*   </u>
which involves bulk shipments in interstate commerce of the product(s)
hereafter named <u>   </u>;

And further that the foregoing shipments be sanctioned by an agreement
made as provided by regulation under section 405, section 503(a), or
section 603 of the Federal Food, Drug, and Cosmetic Act;

Agree that they shall use for the immediate container of such products
the labels specified and provided, as necessary to bring such products into
compliance with said Act before introduction into interstate commerce.

Agree that they shall each keep a copy of this agreement and make such
available for official inspection as required by such regulation.

The customer guarantees that such products are not articles forbidden
entry into interstate commerce under the provisions of section 404 or section 505 of the FFDC Act.

This agreement shall continue until cancelled by either party, on written notice and without prejudice to the other party.

ATTACHMENTS HERETO PART OF THIS AGREEMENT:

Signed for supplier   Signed for customer
<u>*(date)*   (L. S.)</u>   <u>*(date)*   (L. S)*</u>
<u>   (title)</u>   <u>   (title)</u>
<u>   (address)</u>   <u>   (address)</u>

Neither repackager nor his customer need be reluctant to sign agreements
D and E above since they are provided for in the regulations, and actually attach, at least commercially, in the form of warranties according to the Uniform
Sales Act, Uniform Commercial Code, or specific statutes.

Chapter 7

PRODUCTION AND CONTROL RECORDS

21 CFR 133.7   **Master production and control records; batch production
and control records.**

(a) To assure uniformity from batch to batch, a
master production and control record for each drug
product and each batch size of drug product shall
be prepared, dated, and signed or initialed by a
competent and responsible individual and shall be
independently checked, reconciled, dated, and
signed or initialed by a second competent and
responsible individual.

The master formula record that must be prepared for each drug product
describes completely all aspects of its manufacture, packaging, and control.
        According to H. Hammer [*Good Manufacturing Practices,* International
Federation of Pharmaceutical Manufacturers Associations, Zurich, Switzerland,
1971, p. 195], its function is to "insure the purity, identity, quality and
strength of each dosage unit throughout the entire shelf life by:

1. Specifying a fixed formulation.
2. Identifying consistent quality criteria for components.
3. Providing an explicit set of manufacturing instructions.
4. Describing a thorough system of surveillance.
5. Delineating systematic sampling procedures.

6. Listing precise assays and tests.
7. Establishing methods for insuring complete accountability for all material, including packaging and labeling."

It can be of two types:

1. The master formula which gives proportions of ingredients in the formulation.
2. Master batch formula which specifies absolute amounts of specific potent ingredients and excipients.

The master formula is an output of all product design, specification, and control sections. The concept of preparation by one competent individual and independent verification of its correctness with endorsement and dating by both parties is introduced as a basic concept of good manufacturing practice in this section. Competence indicates the possession of sufficient knowledge through academic training and experience to detect any errors in the master formula.

A master formula must exist for each drug produced. Thus, if the company produces different dosage levels of the same active ingredient, each requires a separate master formula, although there might be identical data fields and information in each one.

The master formula should be kept in highly restricted access storage, preferably with one person in charge of its control. This employee should be in a position of sufficient knowledge and authority to coordinate revisions to the formula with federal NDA supplements for each change specified.

The batch formula is derived from the master formula and contains the precise quantity of each ingredient to be used in a single manufacturing cycle. The quantities coincide with equipment capability and capacity. The batch formula is maintained under the same conditions as the master formula.

The following five sections delineate the requirements for the preparation of the master formula.

21 CFR 133.7(a) (1)

*[The master production and control record shall
include:]*
(1) The name of the product, description of the
dosage form, and a specimen or copy of each label

and all other labeling associated with the retail or
bulk unit, including copies of such labeling signed
or initialed and dated by the person or persons
responsible for approval of such labeling.

The product name consists of the manufacturer's trade or proprietary name,
the generic or established name (if different) and the chemical formula.

The dosage form consists of the physical composition of the finished
product as well as the method of administration.

The label is the written, printed, or graphic descriptive information
placed on the product or on the immediate container. Section 502 of the Act
should be consulted for the requirements for label content.

Labeling is all other descriptive material, packaging for the product container, and inserts that accompany the product as a part of integrated shipment into interstate commerce (see 21 CFR 321 k. and 1.).

In Kordell V. U.S. [164 F2d 913 and 335 U.S. 345] it was determined
that labeling may have a variety of meanings. Any printed or verbal claims
relating to a drug product's efficacy or use and which are available to potential
customers may be defined as labeling. Labeling does not have to directly accompany the drug product in interstate commerce or be shipped simultaneously
with the container. An integrated or related transaction with the function of
promotion is sufficient to cause labeling. The company must therefore carefully monitor all types of advertising and correspondence which may allude to
the product to maintain control over labeling and be in conformance with
GMP and the Act.

Labels and labeling copy which are authentic specimens of those used
in production must be attached to the master formula. Photocopies are insufficient in this instance, since colors and paper quality are not apparent.

Master formula labels and labeling serve as the originals against which all
incoming copy, designated for production, is compared prior to release. As
such, they must be kept current, reflecting all changes in dosage levels, indica-
tions, contraindications, administration, warnings, and other information.
The use of sequential revision number prefixes or suffixes on the basic label-
labeling identification code number is strongly recommended to achieve the
desired control.

Current specimens of labels and labeling which are attached to the
master formula must be signed and dated by the person responsible for their
maintenance. Means for determining whether the labels and labeling being
used in production exactly match the sample specimen attached to the master

must be established. Alpha or numerical code designators and machine identifying bars are two alternatives.

21 CFR 133.7(a) (2)

*[The master production and control record shall
include:]*
(2) The name and weight or measure of each active
ingredient per dosage unit or per unit of weight or
measure of the finished drug, and a statement of
the total weight or measure of any dosage unit.

The prudent manufacturer will incorporate each of the following parameters
into the master formula.

1. Absolute weight and weight/weight proportion of each active ingredient
   and each excipient present in the finished product, including:
   a. the target weight or measure of each dosage unit
   b. the target weight or measure of the lot of production
2. The total weight or measure of the finished dosage unit consists of both the
   target weight as well as allowable overage-underage figures which serve as
   upper and lower statistical control limits.

   The control limits for each dosage unit or group of dosage units sampled
should fall well within the official or established specifications to insure conformance to legal requirements.

21 CFR 133.7(a) (3)

*[The master production and control record shall
include:]*
(3) A complete list of ingredients designated by
names or codes sufficiently specific to indicate any
special quality characteristic; an accurate statement
of the weight or measure of each ingredient regardless of whether it appears in the finished product,
except that reasonable variations may be permitted
in the amount of components necessary in the preparation in dosage form provided that provisions for
such variations are included in the master production

and control record; an appropriate statement concerning any calculated excess of an ingredient; an
appropriate statement of theoretical weight or
measure at various stages of processing; and a statement of the theoretical yield.

Each ingredient entering the production cycle must be specified either by name
or by an alpha-numerical code, preferably both, to maintain better control
over raw materials. Distinguishing characteristics must also be specified for
each component. These include weight, particle size variations, crystalline
form, physical or organoleptic distinguishing features, and any qualitative
or quantitative means for reducing error in component selection.

An effective means of assuring ingredient control is to assign each different physical or chemical form of an ingredient a separate specific code designator, i.e., each salt form, crystal form, or different degree of hydration of an
ingredient has a separate item number. To reduce error in selection and usage,
the code designator is used as the primary identifier, the label name is used as
a secondary identifier, and the distinguishing characteristics as an additional
check. When material is selected for issue by the pharmacy function, both
code designator and label name are checked by the person performing the
operation and independently by another qualified employee or supervisor.

Specific weight or measure of each ingredient entering the production
cycle must be made to insure that each batch possesses the same attributes of
purity, identity, strength, and quality. To prevent error, all weights should be
in units of the same system, that is, metric, English or apothecary systems
should be used throughout and the systems should not be mixed. Ideally,
only one unit, such as grams, should be used throughout, with consistent
policy as to use of zeros and decimal points. An untried idea is to use three
weight columns labeled respectively kilograms, grams, and milligrams.

Variation in the amount of specific components added is permitted so
long as the tolerances for these differences are included in the master
formula. The conditions which warrant these variations being used in manufacturing processes must also be identified. These variations are normally
included so that active drug raw materials not assaying at 100% potency may
be adjusted in quantity to compensate for sub- or superpotency. The potency
of the material utilized must be specified and the calculations for determining
the adjusted amount should be shown on the batch formula record. Raw
materials whose potency deviates by more than 10% from that specified are
usually not used.

To effect this adjustment properly it is necessary to perform a quantitative assay regularly on all active ingredients as a part of raw materials control and assign an expiration date based on their stability.

Theoretical yields for the batch at the completion of various in-process manufacturing steps must be specified in the master batch formula. Reconciliation of actual with theoretical yield determinations should be specified after each operation in which raw material components are added to processing and before work-in-process is transferred from the control of one department to another. Theoretical yields are equal to the cumulative total amounts of all ingredients in the formula, less solvent evaporation or amounts removed after the completion of one operation. Determination of actual yield is necessary in order to control the amount entering the next manufacturing process and to make accurate accountability determinations.

21 CFR 133.7(a) (4)

[The master production and control record shall
include:]
(4) A description of the containers, closures, and
packaging and finishing materials.

These descriptions include the complete descriptions of all containers and closures which are in contact with the product as well as all components accompanying the packaged product when distributed.

The container and closure also includes items such as the cotton plug placed in the top of bottles, air seals between the container opening and screw top, plastic shrink seals placed around the closure to prevent air entry, and the metal coverings around rubber closures of parenteral vials.

Data fields required for complete description of each product, including different dosage levels and forms, consist of:

1. Name and part number.
2. Composition.
3. Dimensions—amount used.
4. Color.
5. Special treatments or processes conducted on item.

Packaging and finishing materials are all other items utilized to display and protect the product during shipment and storage. These cartons, packers, packer liners, and separators, staples, tape, and all other components that accompany the product in interstate commerce must be accurately described by:

1. Name and part number.
2. Composition.
3. Dimensions.
4. Weight.
5. Amount used.
6. Where used.

21 CFR 133.7(a) (5)

[The master production and control record shall
include:]
(5) Manufacturing and control instructions, procedures, specifications, special notations and
precautions to be followed.

Manufacturing and control instructions must include all operations from the
dispensing of the product raw materials through the finishing of bulk product
and packaging operations.

    The master batch formula must describe fully all operations required
to manufacture a drug product. It is the primary source of information and
communication from the scientists who formulated the finished dose form
to the numerous operators who must reproduce the same drug product on a
mass production scale. It must thus insure both reproducibility and control
of the drug and the labeled retail package from batch to batch.

    The design of the batch formula sheet should facilitate its being
completed by operators and supervisors during production operations. Specific
information requirements should be stated and sufficient space allotted to
complete the required responses, for example:

        Blend for 20 minutes in pony mixer at 40 rmp
        Machine number: _____
        Time in: _____
        Time out: _____
        Completed by: _____

    Manufacturing instructions are ordered by the sequence in which they
occur during processing and describe completely the operation to be accomplished. These include:

1. The operation to be performed.
2. Ingredients to be added—name and number.

3.   Amount of each ingredient.
4.   Sequence in which ingredients are to be added.
5.   Elapsed time for each operation performed.
6.   Equipment to be utilized—filters, screens, etc.—by designated name and number.
7.   Speed of equipment during processing.
8.   In process manufacturing controls utilized [see 21 CFR 133.8(e)].
9.   Tolerances and standards for weights and measures.
10. Special precautions and hazardous conditions which exist and necessary safety equipment to be utilized.
11. Packaging components and materials—name and number.
12. Label and labeling components, including code for current revision.
13. Packaging sequences performed.
14. Equipment used.
15. Required samples for retention, assay, and process inspection.
16. Protocol for final release.
17. Stability data for packaged dosage form.
18. Spaces for names of operators and supervisor for each operation.
19. Spaces for date of completion of each operation.
20. Spaces for supervisory commentary and results of investigations.

21 CFR 133.7(b)

[Batch production and control records]
(b) The batch production and control record shall be prepared for each batch of drug produced and shall include complete information relating to the production and control of each batch. These records shall be retained for at least 2 years after the batch distribution is complete or at least 1 year after the batch expiration date, whichever is longer. These records shall identify the specific labeling and lot or control numbers used on the batch and shall be readily available during such retention period.

The batch production and control record follows every production batch through the plant. It provides a detailed description of all processing operations and controls, when they are performed, by whom, and where.
    Production and control operations occur at different locations

within the plant. The batch records which accompany material through processing provide information for operators and also serve as a means for documenting which ingredients were added, which control measures were exercised in process, final assay of the drug product, and the huge amount of information produced during the manufacturing cycle. Because this flow of information accompanies the product through all operations, the medium of transmission must be durable and provide protection for the forms which it encloses. Since it is advisable to keep the manufacturing and production portions of the batch record together during these operations, many manufacturers keep batch records for a single production cycle consolidated in a polyethylene bag. To minimize handling and possibility of loss, laboratory records for the batch may be added just prior to release review by the control section. In addition to the information that is attached to the batch production record, the departments contributing to the manufacturing cycle must retain accurate records of material inputs and outputs, processes performed, results, and comments about operations within the department.

The completed batch production record is a legal document and must be retained a minimum of two years following the completion of distribution from all company warehouses, or one year after the expiration date, whichever is longer.

It is not deemed sufficient that the production and control records for a released batch are correctly completed if they are not available for rapid retrieval from archives. This section suggests that all completed records associated with a single batch of production be consolidated and filed so as to insure ready access. Since this section also states that an identifying control number be assigned to each individual batch, this number could serve as the means of indexing these record files.

There is no single correct method for assigning control or lot numbers to production batches. Many larger companies utilize a production planning function which coordinates market requirements, inventory levels, and projected manufacturing necessities. This function may assign control numbers sequentially to the batch formulae as released to production, or each product may have a block of control numbers assigned to it over a specific time period. The former method permits a general idea of when the product was manufactured; the latter indicates how many batches of a specific product have been processed. Both are compatible with the first in-first out method of inventory control.

21 CFR 133.7(b) (1)

[The batch record shall include:]
(1) An accurate reproduction of the appropriate
master formula record, checked, dated, and
signed or initialed by a competent and responsible individual.

The instructions, procedures, controls and specifications established in the
master batch formula must be duplicated to serve as a guide for the actual
production operations.

Accurate duplication may be achieved by copying the master by hand,
mimeographing, photocopying, or computer-printout methods. Copying the
master for each production batch manually is generally less accurate and less
economical, therefore, the last three methods are recommended. The volume
of operations and equipment are the ultimate determinants between the
alternatives.

Although the necessity for the checking of automated copying has
been questioned, errors can occur when the copy is blurred, contains extraneous specks, or is partly cut off. Each page of each copy, therefore, must
be checked, dated, and endorsed by an individual able to detect any error,
usually a department supervisor, before manufacturing operations may commence. This may be done within each production department or by the
control function by direct comparison with a verified copy of the master.

21 CFR 133.7(b) (2)

[The batch record shall include:]
(2) A record of each significant step in the manufacturing, processing, packaging, labeling, testing
and controlling of the batch, including: Dates,
individual major equipment and lines employed;
specific identification of each batch of components used; weights and measures of components
and products used in the course of processing;
in-process and laboratory-control results; and
identification of the individual(s) actively performing and the individual(s) directly supervising or
checking each significant step in the operation.

As mentioned, the batch production formula serves as the medium for recording all processes and procedures which are required in pharmaceutical production. Because a variety of organizational designs is possible, the formula itself may be divided into separate sections to facilitate its flow through the areas of different functional control. Each company may develop and modify the methods which it utilizes to maintain its batch production records without altering the intent of the requirement. As long as accurate, orderly, and efficient records are maintained during production so that they may be assembled at the conclusion of production, the system itself is operable.

The preceding discussion of 21 CFR 133.7(a) stated information requirements which should be included in the batch formula per se. In addition, other information must be attached to or accompany the batch formula so that good manufacturing practices are achieved. These include, but are not limited to:

1. Labels from the transfer containers of all raw materials and components entering the production cycle attached to batch formula as material is added, or some other means of recording:
   a. name and number of each component
   b. amount added
   c. control number assigned to each lot of raw material
   d. date of weighing
   e. person performing weighing
   f. person who checked weight
2. All processing equipment utilized and certification of its cleanliness.
3. Space utilized for operation.
4. Operator's signature for each step.
5. Supervisor's signature for each step.
6. Dates for each step.
7. Control charts.
8. Drying logs indicating time and temperature.
9. In-process tests performed and results, e.g., pH, leakers, visual inspections.
10. Samples taken (finished, in-process goods)—number, time of withdrawal, sampler's name.
11. Theoretical versus actual yield reconciliations.

Emphasis is directed to the requirement that each operation requires both the signature of the person performing the sequence and the supervisor who independently verifies that the manufacturing step was carried out as directed in the batch formula. This division into "doers" and "checkers", each of whom certifies that a stated procedure was actually performed, is fundamental to the entire concept of pharmaceutical quality control.

21 CFR 133.7(b) (3)

[The batch record shall include:]
(3) A batch number that identifies all the production and control documents relating to the history of the batch and all lot or control numbers associated with the batch.

Several concepts requiring explanation are expressed in this subsection. Each batch of material being produced must be assigned a number which serves as the primary means of control, identification, location, and determination of ultimate disposition. Often a production lot is assigned a multiunit alphanumerical code and each batch of the lot is consecutively numbered or lettered.

It is important that the control numbers of all material entering the manufacturing sequence be permanently recorded as having been assigned to the particular lot or batch number. This facilitates the determination of material accountability and serves also as an input for cost accounting. Once the lot-batch number is assigned to a production lot, it also serves as the primary means of identifying the drug during in-process and release analyses by the quality control laboratory.

All analyses performed for the drug product by the control laboratories are entered in the internal records of the laboratory by the lot-batch number assigned to that particular unit of production and the name and number of the product.

The second part of the subsection requires that all lot or control numbers appearing on the labels of drugs from any batch must be traceable to laboratory control procedures. An inference exists that the manufacturing lot-batch number might not coincide with the control number on the packaged material.

If a single lot of bulk manufactured product is utilized in more than one packaging order, the production batch formula should list:

1. Each packaging order to which bulk product is assigned.
2. Packaging control numbers, if different.
3. Quantity utilized in each order.
4. Date of each packaging operation.

Conversely, completion of large quanity packaging orders may require product from more than one production lot. If this condition exists, the permanent packaging records must list each lot or batch number of product utilized to fill it. A method must also be devised to indicate when each different production batch entered the packaging sequence and to permit accountability determinations of the total amounts used. Two systems used are:

1. Separate packaging control numbers may be started each time new bulk product from a different batch or lot enters the finishing cycle. This method has the disadvantage of possibly fragmenting the packaging order into two or more control numbers.
2. A single control number assigned to a packaging order may be augmented with an alpha or numerical prefix or suffix designator each time new bulk product bearing to a different lot or batch number is used. This system is amenable to finishing operations which stencil packaging control numbers on labels and labeling during the operation.

The intent is to insure that, in the event of recall, all product subject to the recall may be removed from the market expeditiously. This requires that permanent batch records for both manufacturing and finishing show and cross-reference which lots and batch numbers were assigned to a packaging control number and which finishing control numbers were filled by bulk material from a single lot or batch. Each number also serves as a means for locating laboratory records for test and assay data. Because of the complexity of control number assignment, prevention of intermingling of product from two different lots, and annoyance in locating a modified control code on a wholesaler or pharmacy shelf, the practice of filling a packaging order with material from more than one lot, while permissible, is not recommended.

Numerical Material Identification Systems

In the previous sections, the concepts of incoming goods being assigned a numerical designator for control purposes, in-process material receiving another, and finally the possibility of packaging goods being assigned still another was described. At this point, it might be useful to more fully describe a pharmaceutical alpha-numerical ordering system.

1. All incoming raw materials, components, and supplies have *item numbers*.

Source: Purchasing—material specifications.

Function: To identify the material by type and specific characteristics.

2. All received raw materials (active ingredients and excipients) are assigned a sequential *control* or *stock number.* One stock number for each discrete vendor lot received,

Source: Receiving department.

Function: To provide accountability and a means for identifying and controlling different received vendor's lot. Each lot is assumed to be homogeneous.

3. A *lot-batch number* is assigned to each scheduled manufacturing cycle for a given product. The lot number may be divided into several batches depending on equipment capacity.

Source: Production planning.

Function: a. to maintain control and accountability over each production cycle

b. to identify separate production cycle output, for permanent records of the control laboratory and the packaging function

4. *Product numbers* are assigned to each different pharmaceutical product possessing substantially identical characteristics. Thus, each separately manufactured and packaged lot of a given product produced by a single manufacturer bears the same product number.

Source: Production planning.

Function: To provide alternative and redundantly duplicative means of product identification both internal and external to the firm's operations.

5. *Packaging control numbers* are designated for each packaging order to provide a means of identifying and specifying the manufactured lot-batch numbers utilized in the operation in order to control the product during marketing. With the requirement for dating pharmaceutical products, the control number provides a means of identifying the age of the drug. Conspicuously placed control numbers on the packaging carton also permit greater specificity in the event of product recall and permit greater control of the distribution process.

Source: Production planning.

Function: To provide greater control over the finished product during and following distribution process.

21 CFR 133.7(b) (4)

[The batch record shall include:]
(4) A record of any investigation made according
to § 133.8(h).

Section 133.8(h) requires supervisory review, comment, and satisfactory
resolution of any discrepancy or deviation from the standards prescribed
in the master formula. Further, any previous lot or batch of the drug
which might have been subjected to a similar variation from specified standards must be identified and reconciled before the drug may be released into
interstate commerce for marketing purposes.

Supervisory commentary should include:

1. Description of the problem.
   a. specific standard exhibiting variance and amount
   b. where discovered
   c. when determined
   d. extent of problem within the lot and other lots possibly affected
2. Commentary on its seriousness in relation to possible adulteration of finished product. (The quality control function should be notified if problem appears likely to result in adulteration or misbranding.)
3. Satisfactory method of rework or salvage, if applicable.
4. Corrective action taken within department for subject lot and investigation made of other possibly affected lots.
5. Supervisor's signature and date of investigation.

This commentary may either be placed directly on the batch formula
or on a separate sheet which is attached to the formula.

Chapter 8

PRODUCTION AND CONTROL PROCEDURES

21 CFR 133.8   Production and control procedures.

Production and control procedures shall include all
reasonable precautions, including the following, to
assure that the drugs produced have the safety, identity, strength, quality, and purity they purport to
possess.

Management, supervisory, and quality control functions should audit, inspect,
and review pharmaceutical production sequences and provide checks to minimize human error, equipment-caused sources of excess variability, and conditions which result in a finished product not possessing its purported purity,
identity, strength, or quality. The control measures taken during the individual production operations will define how well sources of nonrandom variation and preventable error have been identified. The quality of work-in-process
and finished goods demonstrates how well they have been controlled.
     Written instructions for operators and guides for supervisory personnel
which define a scientifically-based set of production standards must be made
for all in-process operations. These must be consistent with those delineated
in the master formula and batch production records, and must conform to
those developed during the research and development phases of the drug.
Controls must insure that the product is in compliance with approved and established standards of fitness both within each lot and on a lot-to-lot basis.

21 CFR 133.8(a)

(a) Each significant step in the process, such as
the selection, weighing, and measuring of components, the addition of ingredients during the
process, weighing and measuring during various
stages of the processing, and the determination
of the finished yield, shall be performed by a
competent and responsible individual and
checked by a second competent and responsible
individual; or if such steps in the processing are
controlled by precision automatic, mechanical,
or electronic equipment, their proper performance is adequately checked by one or more
competent and responsible individuals. The
written record of the significant steps in the
process shall be identified by the individual performing these tests and by the individual
charged with checking these steps. Such iden-
tifications shall be recorded immediately following the completion of such steps.

The concept of "doers and checkers" provides assurance that at certain critical junctures in production operations, the likelihood of human error will
be significantly reduced. If each of these predetermined steps is performed
by a knowledgeable and competent person, and an equally competent
second employee independently verifies that successful completion has occurred, management can easily justify the additional expense of the checker
with the knowledge that the proper amounts of the proper ingredients are
in process.

Doers and checkers may be replaced in certain weighing, measuring,
or identification operations by precision automated equipment. Bulk weighing, tablet identification, weighing, color, and size sorters are examples of
such replacement. Several quality control criteria should be considered by
management, production, and engineering functions before this substitution
occurs.

1. The machine must be designed specifically or modified sufficiently to
   perform the function properly.
2. The machine must be tested and the results shown to be statistically
   equivalent or superior to manual operations.
3. The designated function is completed both accurately and precisely according to preestablished standards.

4. The machines or instruments are regularly standardized, checked, and tested before in-process use.
5. This information is maintained in a permanent departmental log for each piece of equipment.
6. The equipment log must contain and the equipment must be labeled with last date of calibration and frequency of calibration necessary for proper operation.

Critical and sensitive operations are best determined by each manufacturer assessing the scope and nature of his operations and the past history of performance. A high incidence of any particular error in the production cycle that is attributable to a single operation would cause that sequence to become significant.

The following are usually critical operations for any manufacturing concern:

1. The selection from stock, identification, weighing or measuring, and reconciliation of active ingredients and excipients in the raw materials issuance department.
2. The addition of these raw materials during production operations.
3. Completion of critical in-process manufacturing operations by each of the various departments involved. This includes mixing, comminuting, lubricating, compressing, encapsulating, film coating, polishing, filtering liquids, filling.
4. Review of in-process manufacturing controls as designated in the batch formula.
5. Approval of punch and die sets for installation in presses for compressed tablets. Supervisory approval should include examination of tablets from each punch and die assembly before approval is given for a production run.
6. Final weight determinations for reconciling theoretical with actual yields in each department. Each lot of manufactured material and raw materials entering production should be identified, and the weights, as determined by weighers and checkers, compared to weights listed on the accompanying master batch formula by a supervisor. This sequence should be completed by both the department completing the manufacturing operation and the department receiving the material for the next sequence.

Verification by both the employee performing the operation and by the checker to determine satisfactory completion of the operation is required.

This necessitates use of record forms so that these signatures and dates may be written legibly. Signatures then become a part of permanent records of each manufactured lot or batch.

21 CFR 133.8(b)

(b) All containers, lines, and equipment used during the production of a batch of a drug shall be properly identified at all times to accurately and completely indicate their contents and, when necessary, the stage of processing of the batch.

The inclusion of this requirement suggests that a suitable means of reproducing sufficient quantities of semipermanent labels for all containers used to store and transport both work in process and finished bulk material, as well as the equipment utilized for production, must be available to the manufacturer. One method of doing this for large scale operations is by an automated printer attached to a computer. The labels are printed in the same sequence as the master batch formula and included in the packet when it is transferred to production. If the scale of operations is not sufficient to warrant off-line facilities, mimeograph masters may be prepared and duplicated easily. Adhesive labels with peel backing are easily handled and processed by both types of duplicating equipment. The labels should be large enough to read easily and contain sufficient space to accommodate the following data fields:

1. Product name and number.
2. Lot number—batch number.
3. Total quantity of containers in batch—individual container number.
4. Quantity contained in individual container.
5. Operator's signature—checker's where appropriate.
6. Date
7. Last operation completed.

Data fields (1) and (2) may be preprinted on the label, the remainder filled in as operations are completed. When there is more than one drum per batch, each drum should be numbered sequentially as filled to increase accountability. In addition, when rotary compressing machines with more than one ejection side are used, the drum label must be able to indicate which side of the machine compressed the tablet. This information may be cross-referenced to a control chart maintained for the machine. "Last operation completed" may be applied to the label with a rubber stamp at the time it is affixed to the drum.

Other quality control necessities include:

1. Container tare weight with lid and liner affixed to drum before use.
2. All equipment in use properly identified with data fields (1) through (3) inclusive.
3. All affixed identification removed, or if not possible, completely obliterated when container is emptied.
4. Only containers being utilized in processing or filled with product shall be labeled. No containers should be prelabeled before actual use.
5. All containers for each lot and batch are numbered consecutively.
6. Operation being conducted is stamped on the container label.
7. Containers containing waste material, samples, scrap, etc., must be prominently labeled to indicate contents.
8. Containers being utilized as a supply source for continuous operations (e.g., drums of granulation for compressing or encapsulation, liquid filling operations) should be marked "Approved for [operation]" by supervisory personnel before being used.
9. All containers must be labeled outside on the container side and lid. If a label will not contaminate the product, a label also should be placed inside the container. All labels contain data fields (1) through (7) inclusive.

If operations are being conducted in a room, booth, or partitioned cubicle, this area must also be identified. Recommended is a multipurpose identification tag which indicates the operational sequence being conducted in the space being used, the product and lot number being processed, the date of processing and the following:

1. Assurance of room cleanliness.
2. Assurance of equipment cleanliness.
3. Assurance of correct materials being used.
4. Supervisor's signature and date.

Tags preprinted with the indicated data fields may be completed in each department before operations begin.

This completed form should be included as part of the permanent batch record to evidence compliance with stringent operating and control procedures.

21 CFR 133.8(c), (d)

(c) To minimize contamination and prevent mix-ups, equipment, utensils, and containers shall be thoroughly and appropriately cleaned and properly stored and have previous batch identification removed or obliterated between batches or at suitable intervals in continuous production operations.

(d) Appropriate precautions shall be taken to minimize microbiological and other contamination in the production of drugs purporting to be sterile or which by virtue of their intended use should be free from objectionable microorganisms.

The emphasis of these two paragraphs is the cleanliness of the equipment and containers which are utilized in production operations. Sterility is the minimum standard for cleanliness in the production of parenterals or ophthalmics. X. Buhlman [*Pharm. Acta Helv.,* **46**, 385-410 (1971)], defines sterility of these products as freedom from viable or dead microorganisms, pyrogens, enzymes or other foreign material.

In the case of nonsterile products, cleanliness is attained by the use of hot water, detergent, and steam baths when possible, on all equipment. Materials which are nonreactive and able to withstand vigorous high-velocity water and high-temperature cleanings are required. Stainless steel, although initially expensive, remains the preferred material for most heavy equipment and machinery. High-density polymers have numerous applications as utensils. Materials which tend to fragment, chip, blister, or are chemically additive to or reactive with the drug must be avoided.

Exact washing cycles must be determined for all pieces of equipment, with consideration of both the material used for the equipment and the drug component it contained during the manufacturing process. Swab tests should be performed to insure freedom from residues of drug and detergent when washing cycles are being established. Once determined, cycles must be strictly followed. After washing and drying cycles, each piece of equipment should be covered either with its lid or a secured piece of plastic. All equipment should be rinsed immediately before use.

Permanently placed equipment, especially modular and sequential operation machinery such as ribbon blenders, tanks, mills, and mixers, present special problems since they are large, cumbersome, and frequently difficult or impossible to disassemble. As with portable equipment, procedures to insure cleanliness must be carefully defined and rigidly followed. The equipment must be disassembled whenever possible for a more complete cleaning process. Permanently placed equipment should have a log which specifies the exact washing procedure and cycle times that is maintained for both product and lot change-overs. Relevant data fields for the washing process included in this log are:

1. Person performing cleaning.
2. Date.
3. Supervisor's signature of cleanliness check.

Equipment records included in the completed batch production record include the equipment cleanliness record, and the room, booth, or cubicle identification card which shows the product run, lot and batch numbers, supervisor's signature, and date.

Ultrasonic cleaners may be effectively employed for small parts on precision equipment, such as punches.

The procedures for sterile equipment are more involved and critical. In addition to the normal washing procedures, sterility must be insured for certain containers and equipment used in manufacturing and filling operations. Terminal sterilization of the product is not an acceptable substitute for proper cleanliness of manufacturing components, equipment and utensils.

1. Containers used for holding sterile products must be sterilized and show date of sterilization.
2. Components coming in contact with sterile products must be sterilized and show the date of sterilization.
3. Sterilized equipment or components should be used within three days of sterilization.
4. Sterilized equipment should be replaced between consecutive lot numbers of the same product to maintain control number integrity.
5. Sterilization (Dyak) indicators should be used with equipment to show completion of the sterilization cycle. [See also 21 CFR 133.11(e) (1).]

The requirement for label and identification removal or obliteration from equipment following their use, when combined with an in-house policy of prompt removal from production to a wash area, greatly reduces the possibility for drug cross-contamination.

If the same equipment is to be utilized for processing several batches of the same production lot number, identification does not have to be removed between batches, but must properly indicate the batch being currently processed. For example, more than one batch may be granulated separately and combined later during a mixing step to form a homogeneous lot when larger capacity equipment may be employed. It is necessary, however, that this procedure be carefully defined in the master and batch production records and that uniform raw materials stock be used.

Equipment which operates on a continuous production basis should have batch numbers assigned on a time basis. Any convenient time sequence is acceptable as long as the raw materials entering the production cycle are from the same lot number and identical procedures are followed. A shift-to-shift change is frequently utilized.

21 CFR 133.8(e)

(e) Appropriate procedures shall be established to minimize the hazard of cross-contamination of any drugs while being manufactured or stored.

Some of the procedures which are intended to reduce the opportunity for product cross-contamination have been specified in previous sections of Good Manufacturing Practices. Management must determine where different ingredients, both active and excipients, may come in contact with contaminants. Procedures, specifications, equipment, or plant alterations must then be formulated to prevent this occurrence.

Some important considerations are:

1. All raw materials should be received from vendors in previously unused containers.
2. Containers should be intact and of sufficient strength to prevent escape of raw materials.
3. Containers designed to permit a tight reclosure following sampling and use—outer surfaces cleaned by vacuum after use.
4. Containers of raw materials tightly closed when not in use.

5. Raw materials segregated by vendors' lot numbers during storage.
6. All raw materials weighed and dispensed in segregated booths.
7. Raw materials for one lot or batch number dispensed at one time.
8. Weighed raw materials placed in separate containers. These containers may be consolidated into one or more sealed containers for shipment to manufacturing.
9. Clean and nonporous, nonreactivie instruments used for weighing or transferring raw materials.
10. Materials from one lot adequately separated from others; i.e., not in same production room, booth, or cubicle, or when stored, one foot space between different lots or drums stored on separate pallets.
11. All containers for bulk product cleaned thoroughly before use; fiberboard containers contain clean polyethylene liner folded over edge.
12. Containers and equipment being used in production operations covered whenever possible contamination might occur, e.g., during breaks, whenever container not being filled or emptied during operation of equipment.
13. All containers sealed after filling.
14. Proper cleaning procedures used on all production equipment before use.
15. Clean equipment used to manufacture a single production lot only.
16. Production area clean, neat, and orderly at all times.
17. Dust control equipment in operation during production.
18. Dirt, dust, or product spills vacuumed immediatley. Oils, grease, and all materials not involved in operations cleaned with disposable rags or wipes.
19. Supply containers closed until processing begins.
20. Supply containers removed from area immediately after emptying.
21. All packaging equipment cleaned of product before use. Tablet counters and fillers disassembled and cleaned between packaging different products.
22. All product kept within limits of packaging area.
23. Separate packaging areas segregated by walls or partitions.

21 CFR 133.8(f)

(f) To assure the uniformity and integrity of products, there shall be adequate in-process controls such as checking the weights and disintegration time of tablets, the adequacy of mixing, the homogeneity of suspensions and the clarity of solutions. In-process sampling shall be done at appropriate intervals using suitable equipment.

In-process controls are of two types: (1) those that are performed by production personnel at the time of operation to insure that machinery is producing output within preestablished control limits; (2) those performed by the quality control laboratory personnel to insure compliance to official compendial or in-house specifications prior to further processing or release for distribution.

In-process manufacturing controls are established by quality control and production personnel to insure that a predictable percentage of each output cycle falls within the acceptable tolerance standards determined during the product development phase. Failure to adhere to these parameters may result in the drug being deemed adulterated under section 501(b).

To insure proper statistical significance for any in-process control, the following must be defined:

1. Process to be sampled and at what phase.
2. Number of samples to be taken during the process and frequency of sampling.
3. Quantity included in each sample.
4. A target or optimum value for the product and sample to serve as the mean around which a distribution will fall.
5. Allowable variability for statistical control limits.

Although the production output may not follow a pure normal distribution, there is enough similarity that its laws are applicable and amenable for analysis. The five requirements insure that the samples will be representative of the lot so that unwarranted conclusions concerning its quality will not be made. The sampling procedures as defined in the United States Military Standard 105-D at Levels I and II are easily implemented and provide uniformity for sampling procedures.

Controls are defined by the attributes considered critical to product quality. Frequency of sampling is defined by economics, since all product between the last satisfactory check and an unsatisfactory check is suspect. Recommended frequencies are based on usual production rates. Manufacturing in-process controls include, but are not limited to, the following tests:

1. Granulation moisture determinations—once per batch.
2. Disintegration times of tablets and capsules—twice each shift.

3. Capsule or tablet weight—individual and group weights—every 15 minutes.

The following parameters should be determined before resuming manufacturing following any period of shut down and every fifteen minutes during operations.

1. Tablet thickness—minimum of five tablets.
2. Tablet hardness and friability.
3. Weight and specific gravity checks of suspensions.
4. Clarity, color, pH, specific gravity of solutions.
5. Adequacy of mixing or dispersion.
6. Fill of liquids or ointments.
7. Visual or organoleptic defects—foreign matter, capping, mottling, spots, poor print, coating or coloring irregularities.

Appropriate control charts, with average and range data fields, for each of these items must be maintained by production and included with the batch production formula as part of the permanent records for each lot.

Control charts must show:

1. Product name and number.
2. Lot number.
3. Batch number.
4. Container number being processed when sample taken.
5. Date.
6. Operator.
7. Target and minimum-maximum specifications as established by the master formula.

These control charts are to be completed as tests are made by the operator and kept at the machine site.

Before operations are started provision should be made for segregating samples from the production run which will be used to judge the quality of the output. Provision should also be made for segregating and appropriately labeling output that does not meet control specifications.

During production operators may adjust machinery to maintain output within tolerances. Adjustment should be made only when the output varies more than 5% from the target value. Two successive tests with product outside of specification tolerances should be brought to the supervisor's attention for possible product quarantine.

The equipment being utilized for in-process control checks must be operating correctly.

1. Hardness testers checked weekly.
2. Balances and thickness gauges zeroed prior to each measurement.
3. Disintegration baths temperature at 37°C.
4. Color measuring devices standardized after shutdown or interruption in operations, checked every 30 minutes during production.

21 CFR 133.8(g)

(g) Representative samples of all dosage form drugs shall be tested to determine their conformance with the specifications for the product before distribution.

The language plainly indicates that the samples shall be of the finished product ready for distribution. Laboratory examination of the product for conformance with all specifications includes not only appropriate tests and assays but also visual inspection for defects and a check of all labeling against master copy.

Representative samples are obtained by removing samples from production at equal intervals throughout the entire production cycle. The samples tested should reflect output from the beginning, middle, and end of the manufacturing sequence.

21 CFR 133.8(h)

(h) Procedures shall be instituted whereby review and approval of all production and control records, including packaging and labeling, shall be made prior to the release or distribution of a batch. A thorough investigation of any unexplained discrepancy or the failure of a batch to meet any of its specifications shall be undertaken whether or not the batch has already been distributed. This investigation shall be undertaken by a competent and responsible individual and shall extend to other batches of the same drug and other drugs that may have been associated with the specific

failure. A written record of the investigation shall
be made and shall include the conclusions and
followup.

The requirement of review and approval of all production and control
records prior to release of distribution is rather nebulous as to when and by
whom it is to be accomplished. An efficient and economical method which
seems to meet the requirements is review and approval by departmental
supervisory personnel prior to release to the next sequence in the manufacturing cycle. It also seems possible to distribute a batch of drug whose
batch record shows unexplained discrepancies and failure to meet some
specifications.

The law seems weak here. Although material not meeting all in-house
specifications might still meet all legal requirements and present no health
hazard, good manufacturing practices dictate that a single competent
authority should review and approve all production and control records as
a whole before reaching a decision to release a batch for distribution.

Review of raw materials issued should include checks for:

1. Utilization of correct components. (Attach component labels to batch
   formula.)
2. Weighing of correct amounts.
3. Correct labeling of components.
4. All components "in-date" for quality and potency.

Accountability determinations for ascertaining the amount of material
lost during processing or which possibly never was included as a material
input must be made at the conclusion of each primary manufacturing step.
These include but are not limited to:

1. Granulating–post lubrication.
2. Tableting.
3. Encapsulation.
4. Film coating.
5. Sorting.
6. Liquid manufacturing during filtration.
7. Semisolid manufacturing.
8. Liquid filling.

Theoretical weight consists of the summation of the weights of all raw materials entering the production cycle within the operation of concern. For granulations and powders, an amount equal to evaporated solvent should be subtracted from the above figure. Accountability is to be determined for each batch of every lot of production to insure a high degree of materials control.

The term "unexplained discrepancy" for accountability requires managerial decisions as to expected losses. Inputs to the final decision must be governed by the physical properties of the material (light in weight or dense so that little is lost through the air), the number of operations through which all material is processed (comminuting, tableting, encapsulation, and grinding have high loss rates) and, of course, past histories of product loss in the same operational sequence.

A point which must be remembered is that any material recovered from the operation, although not in the finished form, has been accounted for. This includes waste tablets, samples, granulation collected from de-dusters or vacuum systems, and liquids remaining in vats, transfer pipes, and filling machines. Whenever spills occur, production personnel must immediately advise supervisors so that they may enter this amount in the production records as an accountable loss.

$$\% \text{ Loss} = 1 - \left(\frac{\text{total output of production cycle}}{\text{total input to production cycle}} \right) \times 100$$

where

Input	=	(a)	amount received from previous department
		(b)	amount added during departmental operations
Output	=	(a)	finished product continued in process
		(b)	collected waste
		(c)	samples taken [not included in (a)]
		(d)	discarded out-of-specification material

Part of any ongoing quality control program is the computation of a running average for percent losses of each product. Statistical evaluation of these process averages permits the establishment of a target process average as well as tolerance levels. Loss greater than the control level must be investigated and reconciled by supervisory personnel.

Production and control records which must be reviewed and approved by packaging supervisory personnel are described in detail in 21 CFR 10. They include:

1. Correct product packaged and labeled as verified by product code on material and label specimen from bulk drum.
2. Verification of correct packaging, capping, wrapping, and cartoning materials utilized.
3. Label and labeling specimen enclosed with batch production formula.
4. Material, label, and label accountability is satisfactory.
5. Samples retained for stability testing and chemical and microbiological prerelease assay.
6. Control samples examined at predetermined levels during production to determine defect levels.

The functions of quality control laboratories are sufficiently critical to warrant a separate section, 133.11. Prior to market release, chemical and microbiological assays must be performed on all batches and lots of manufactured output to insure compliance to compendial, in-house or advertised claims. Managerial review of laboratory records must be made to insure:

1. Proper analytical methods utilized for the drug substance assayed.
2. All test results meet compendial, in-house or NDA specifications.
3. Retention samples kept for future needs.
4. Assay results included in both departmental records and batch production records.

The quality control section of operations should receive all approved departmental production and control records and laboratory assay results as the final sequence before the release of a lot for distribution. If the documentation demonstrates that all required procedures have been followed, control data recorded, and the product meets necessary standards of pharmaceutical purity, identity, quality, and strength, the quality control function has sole authority to remove it from premarketing quarantine. It is mandatory that material not be released for distribution until positive action has been taken and notification received from this function.

This section also requires a written "investigative history" of those batches which have high loss percentages or fail to meet specifications or deviate in any way from production or control standards. This investigation is to be made by competent personnel, usually from the quality control function.

The written record should include:

1. A statement of the reason for the investigation, that is, how the product differs from that expected.
2. A summation of process sequences or operator techniques which might be responsible for the discrepancy.
3. Corrective actions necessary to be applied to the lot or batch under investigation.
4. Corrective actions necessary to prevent recurrence.
5. Statement of other batches or lots possibly affected and results of their investigation.
6. Statement of other drugs processed at the same time which might be adversely affected and results of their investigation.
7. Comments by the production and quality control functions.
8. Signatures and dates of production and quality control personnel involved.

21 CFR 133.8(i)

(i) Returned goods shall be identified as such and held. If the conditions under which returned goods have been held, stored, or shipped prior to or during their return, or the condition of the product, its container, carton, or labeling as a result of storage or shipping, cast doubt on the safety, identity, strength, quality, or purity of the drug, the returned goods shall be destroyed or subjected to adequate examination or testing to assure that the material meets all appropriate standards or specifications before being returned to stock for warehouse distribution or repacking. If the product is neither destroyed nor returned to stock, it may be reprocessed provided the final product meets all its standards and specifications. Records of returned goods shall be maintained and shall indicate the quantity returned, date, and actual disposition of the product. If the reason for returned goods implicates associated batches, an appropriate investigation shall be made in accordance with the requirements of paragraph (h) of this section.

This section appears self-explanatory and is allowed to stand without further comment.

Production and Control Procedures Not Included in 21 CFR 133.8

Although not mentioned, the phrasing of section 8, Good Manufacturing Practices, implies that there is to be an independently functioning quality control section which monitors the conformance of the production subsystem to written specifications concerning product control. The function of quality assurance with a monitoring overview allows a review of processes and procedures without production relegating its responsibility for meeting standards.

Specific procedural audits to be checked by quality control include:

1. No foreign matter in product or production area.
2. Correct amounts of correct ingredients added.
3. All formula ingredients added to product.
4. Materials from one lot adequately separated from others; i.e., not in the same production room, booth, or cubicle or when stored, one foot space between different lots or drums stored in separate pallets.
5. All materials maintained under specified storage condition.
6. Machine speeds and directions specified in production formula followed.
7. All containers cleaned thoroughly before use; fiberboard containers contain clean or new liner folded over edge. A new polyethylene liner is recommended.
8. Containers and equipment being used in production operations covered whenever possible contamination might occur, e.g., during breaks, whenever container not being filled or emptied during operation of equipment.
9. Containers sealed after filling.
10. Production equipment stored on racks, not placed on floor or machinery.
11. Equipment used to manufacture a single product only (exception: liquid, semisolid or sterile production) cleaned after every fourth cycle.
12. Personnel properly attired for task being performed.
    a. minimum nonsterile requirements: hats, clean work uniforms provided by company every other day; aprons, gloves when handling product; safety shoes, safety glasses, protective goggles and masks.
    b. minimum aseptic requirements:
       (1) workers put on clean uniforms each time the area is entered
       (2) uniforms made of nonlinting material
       (3) all personnel wash their hands with disinfectant before entering the area

      (4) hats worn at all times

      (5) before entering the area workers put on sterile clothing: gowns (long sleeve), hats (designed to prevent all "shedding"), gloves, boots, masks

      (6) the following items prohibited: jewelry, wrist watches, nail polish

      (7) workers queried for colds and other respiratory infections daily

      (8) workers testing positive reassigned to nonsterile jobs

13. Product must agree with all formula specifications.
14. Production area clean, neat, and orderly at all times. Vacuum dirt and dust, remove oil, grease, and all materials not involved in operation.
15. Safety procedures followed.
16. Dust control equipment in operation during production.
17. Supply containers closed until processing begins.
18. Supply containers removed from area immediately after emptying.

Additional Aseptic Area Precautions

1. Positive air pressure, temperature and humidity controls, indicators functioning properly.
2. Laminar flow apparatus functioning properly:
   a. tested annually by manufacturer, installer, or professional service
   b. tested bimonthly by particle counter which detects particles greater than 5 μm.
3. Laminar flow hoods turned on at least one-half hour before use.
4. Laminar flow hoods have adequate shielding surrounding them to prevent nonsterile air from entering sterile area.
5. Culture media exposed near filling dispenser during filling—in other areas on filling line before stoppering.
6. Ultraviolet lights working properly:
   a. energized at all times
   b. located to irradiate critical areas such as entrances
   c. checked for intensity bimonthly
7. Sterility indicators affixed to and inside each sterilizing container for each run.
8. Sterilizing containers for components and product identified with load number, date, contents, by a method that will not be destroyed during the sterilizing cycle.
9. Nonsterile equipment not permitted in aseptic areas.

10. All equipment being used in aseptic filling protected by laminar air flow and adequate shielding.
11. Filling needles covered during periods of non-use and changed between lots or every other day.
12. Air locks used—no open doors between different areas.

Chapter 9

PRODUCT CONTAINERS

21 CFR 133.9 Product containers and their components.

Suitable specifications, test methods, cleaning procedures, and, when indicated, sterilization procedures
shall be used to assure that containers, closures, and
other component parts of drug packages are suitable
for their intended use. Product containers and their
components shall not be reactive, additive or absorptive so as to alter the safety, identity, strength,
quality, or purity of the drug or its components beyond the official or established requirements and
shall provide adequate protection against external
factors that can cause deterioration or contamination of the drug.

Several aspects of container and closure selection, testing, preparation, and
utilization are pertinent when considering associated good manufacturing
practices. Both container and closure are in intimate contact with the
product for extended periods of time under varying conditions. Since no
container or closure available today is completely nonreactive, it is necessary
to test them both in conjunction with the product they will enclose to insure
that there is no physical or chemical interaction which will affect established
drug standards for purity, identity, strength, and quality.
    The determination of the optimum container and closure for a

specific product is primarily a function of research and development. Tests are conducted to measure:

1. Physical and chemical changes which occur in the container and closure under a variety of extreme heat, moisture, and light conditions.
2. Moisture and gas permeability.
3. Reactions and interactions between the drug and the container-closure at conditions of elevated temperatures and humidity.
4. The physical protection provided by the container and closure against impact, motion, pressure, and other stress.
5. Toxicity and stability in animals. Compendial tests are specified for studying these factors for plastic and glass and should be consulted for more complete information.
6. Compatability with automated filling, labeling, and packaging operations (determined with production engineers).

The container-closure assembly which provides the maximum protection against the loss of chemical and pharmaceutical integrity while meeting cost factors should be selected. It is highly desirable to be able to use components which are available as normal stock items from suppliers. This factor assures ready availability and consistency of the product. It becomes necessary to develop custom formulas for containers and closures when stock items do not provide protection against alteration and degradation of the drug dosage form. This situation occurs often with plastics and rubber compounds.

Specifications for Containers and Closures

The product container and closure specifications are prepared jointly by the Research and Development and Quality Control functions. Each lists the chemical and physical characteristics required for a specific component. The master formula lists and cross-references the item numbers of each unit of the required container-closure system for the drug product. This sequential documentation insures that the pharmaceutical is marketed in the same container which meets specific requirements on a batch-to-batch basis.

The specifications include the following items:

1. A description of the component.
2. A statement of chemical composition and method of manufacturing when critical.

3. Size and dimension requirements (gauge, thickness, opening, screw) with target value and acceptable tolerances.
4. Color requirements.
5. Reference to specific manufacturing processes necessary to make the article acceptable to pharmaceutical production (e.g., coating, sterility, printing, washing).
6. Packaging and labeling requirements for shipment to pharmaceutical plant.

It is normally the function of the Quality Control department to review product specifications with the manufacturer or supplier of special product container components. For those items which may be purchased from regular stock, purchasing should review the manufacturing and control practices of the component producer to insure that quality and consistency standards can be met.

An excellent review article pertinent to all primary packaging components is: Jack Cooper, "Quality Control of Plastic Pharmaceutical Containers," *Chron. Pharm.* **14**, 19-27, January 1971.

Internally, these specifications serve as guides for a detailed quality control inspection of each lot of components entering the plant. The information and materials flow involved with container and closure use follows.

1. Purchasing and receiving functions.
    a. purchasing department places order referencing specification requirements where applicable
    b. receiving function inspects incoming shipment for correctness of packaging and labeling and damages
        (1) the shipment is not accepted if any defects are noted, but is returned to the supplier
        (2) if the shipment is accepted, each item is isolated by lot number, and quality control is notified of the arrival so that inspection may be made
    c. copy of container and closure specifications are filed with incoming components inspection department of quality control
    d. purchasing receives reports of defective materials from receiving or quality control, notifies vendor for comment; reviews practices of supplier with possible cancellation of contract if defects not remedied
2. Quality control.
    a. determine bulk container sampling levels based on the number of incoming bulk containers per lot number

    b. determine quantity of individual product containers or enclosures to be examined by components inspection following desired sampling plan (from Military Standard 105 D)

    c. determine critical, major, minor defects and appropriate acceptable quality levels for each type of defect

        (1) critical defects are those which would lead to adulteration or mis-branding of the product and product recall. They also are likely to cause the product to become unfit for use or interfere with operations

            (a) component of incorrect size, gauge, composition

            (b) missing, incorrect, or illegible printing on printed components

Discovery of a critical defect results in rejection of the lot.

        (2) major defects might cause the product to become unfit if used to package the drug and should prevent the product from being distributed

            (a) smeared printing on components

            (b) minor color deviations or finish rejects from specifications

        (3) minor defects are unlikely to cause any product damage or result in the product being unfit for use—they are cosmetically unelegant and relatively inconsequential

            (a) dented, dirty, or scratched components

            (b) torn or folded cartoning

3. Receiving.

    a. assign stock number to incoming goods based on supplier's lot number

    b. segregate by stock number in quarantine area until released by quality control

4. Components inspection.

    a. sample all incoming lots of containers and closures in accordance with pre-determined levels

    b. inspect samples for defective material

        (1) color, shape dimensions, weight, finish

        (2) compendial tests, spectroscopic analysis, heat analysis

        (3) special tests for processes performed, e.g., heat, coating, silicone

        (4) visual defects

    c. accept or reject in accordance with predetermined acceptable quality levels

        (1) accept: tag each bulk container as quality control accepted; move into production sequences

        (2) reject: segregate in quarantine area; return to vendor or separate acceptable from defective

The containers and closures being utilized in the processing of sterile ophthalmic and parenteral products must be sterilized. Containers for parenteral products must be pyrogen-free. Prior to the sterilization cycle, all particulate material must be removed from the containers and closures. Certain coating procedures may be applied during the washing cycle to reduce container and closure reactivity and increase the ease of the stoppering procedure. Once these components have been sterilized it is mandatory that sterility is not lost before use. A maximum time limit between the sterilization process and utilization of the component must be established and vigorously observed. Components should be packed in sealed containers prior to sterilizaton and stored on the clean side of the sterilizer after sterilization and prior to utilization. Seals should be broken only in a sterile environment.

As with other processes, the efficacy of sterilizing and washing procedures must be established and documented. Good Manufacturing Practices then dictates that each washing cycle and each sterilizer load conform to standard procedures. Recording charts and sterility indicators are necessary for this assurance, as are trained and experienced equipment loaders and operators.

The identity of the containers and closures must be maintained throughout all handling procedures by conspicuous identification on containers holding the components. If components are prelabeled, accountability procedures must be followed.

1. Component being processed identified on equipment during washing and sterilizing operations.
2. No more than one component processed on a line at any time.
3. Only distilled or deionized water of proper temperature used in washing cycle.
4. Washed containers and closures placed in proper containers for sterilization.
5. Sterilization processes followed as per standard operating procedures for each bulk container being sterilized.
6. Control and temperature recording charts used for each cycle of the sterilizer.
7. Sterilized components removed to sterile area via sterile room exit.
8. Sterilized components used within three days (ethylene oxide sterilization requires sufficient time to vent residual gas).
9. Bulk container containing sterile components opened and utilized in sterile environment. Proper components used during filling operations.
10. Heat-sealed ampules leak tested.
11. All parenterals subjected to 100% visual inspection by specially selected and trained personnel to remove defective product.

12. Samples submitted to quality control laboratory for microbiological and analytical releases.

Nonsterile Components

1. Proper approved components staged for filling operations.
2. Containers cleaned and inspected prior to filling.

Chapter 10

PACKAGING AND LABELING

21 CFR 133.10   Packaging and labeling.

Packaging and labeling operations shall be adequately
controlled: To assure that only those drug products
that have met the specifications established in their
master production and control records shall be distributed; to prevent mixups between drugs during
filling, packaging, and labeling operations; to assure
that correct labels and labeling are employed for the
drug; and to identify the finished product with a
lot or control number that permits determination
of the history of the manufacture and control of
the batch. An hour, day, or shift code is appropriate as a lot or control number for drug products
manufactured or processed in continuous production equipment.

Good Manufacturing Practices requirements for packaging and labeling are
consistent with the provisions of other sections. The emphasis on control
over materials and products entering this phase of production is obvious.
Control is maintained by:

1. Complete laboratory analysis of the bulk product before release for filling
   operations to insure that it meets master formula specifications.
2. Design and layout of operations to prevent product and package cross-
   contamination.

3. Distribution of the proper amounts of the proper labels, labeling and drug to be used in the packaging operations.
4. The placement of a control number on each product container so that distribution may be regulated.
5. Quarantine following packaging and labeling to permit accountability of product, market packages, labels, and labeling before release.

As with all other aspects of total quality control, certain prerequisites are mandatory.
1. A carefully planned description of all sequences which are to occur in packaging and labeling so that there is minimal opportunity for error.
2. Certification that designated critical steps in these operations did occur must be made in permanent records and documents by persons with knowledge and experience (supervisory personnel). Plans to achieve maximum control may vary from operation to operation.
3. Sufficient personnel (workers, supervisors, inspectors) must be present so that no single person is responsible for more than he is capable of controlling.

These prerequisites are reduced to standard operating policy by written procedures of the packaging and labeling protocols. While the majority of the control procedures are identical for all finishing operations, the components, labels, labeling, environmental conditions, quantity packaged, contract requirements, etc., will vary from lot to lot. Instructions must be sufficiently detailed to prevent production of defective material yet flexible enough to permit necessary variation.

Batch Packaging Formula

This form specifies the packaging and labeling requirements for a single packaged form of a particular dosage unit. It contains the following data fields.

1. Drug product name, number, and strength.
2. Names, item numbers, and descriptions of:
   a. packaging components—bottle, lid, seal
   b. cartoning—spacers, protective packaging
   c. labels
   d. labeling
   e. inserts

3. Complete description of the equipment to be utilized for packaging operations.
4. Special characteristics to be measured and controlled during filling, packaging, and labeling. (e.g., temperature, fill, clarity, pH, specific gravity, color).
5. The number of personnel required to complete packaging-labeling operations. With assembly line setups, this concept is important so that one person does not have more responsibility than he can satisfactorily perform. Enough personnel should be assigned to each line so that at least one member can routinely inspect the finished product for defects.
6. Exact filling, packaging, and labeling requirements and operations described for each person assigned for the operation.
7. Samples required for retention.

This document is product specific, but does not describe the quantity to be processed, the current applicable labeling revisions, lot or packaging control number assigned, and other finishing specific requirements.

Packaging Order

This second document amplifies information so that supplier warehouse and line supervisors can determine specific operational and logistical requirements for each packaging cycle. Relevant data fields include:

1. Packaging lot or control number assigned to particular operation.
2. Lot or batch number of bulk drug product to be filled, packaged, and labeled.
3. Quantity of output desired and amounts of labels, labeling, and packaging components required.
4. Current applicable revision numbers for all components and printed material.
5. Special instructions applicable for a particular operation.

Both documents are combined with other control and quality assurance forms after completion of packaging-labeling operations to form the packaging batch record. Consistent with the requirements of the manufacturing batch records, these should be retained until after complete distribution of stock. In addition, the control number assigned to the packaged output from any single labeling operation must be cross referenced to the batch number of the bulk drug which was finished. In case of recall, this permits rapid and accurate accountability determinations of all suspect material.

21 CFR 133.10(a)

["Packaging and labeling operations shall:]
(a) Be separated (physically or spatially) from
operations on other drugs in a manner adequate
to avoid mixups and minimize cross-contamination.
Two or more packaging or labeling operations
having drugs, containers, or labeling similar in
appearance shall not be in process simultaneously
on adjacent or nearby lines unless these operations are separated either physically or spatially.

The physical segregation barriers and design requirements necessary for packaging operations were described in 21 CFR 133.3. To reiterate briefly:

1. A physical barrier which extends the complete length between adjacent packaging lines.
2. Personnel segregation to prevent persons other than packaging personnel assigned to the line, movers of finished goods, supervisory, and quality control inspection personnel in the immediate packaging areas.
3. Product segregation insured by:
   a. adequate space for prepackaging staging within the demarcated packaging line
   b. no commingling of product, packaging components, or labeling between lines
   c. prompt removal of finished, inspected market packages from lines

Packaging operations that fully comply to the intent of Good Manu-facturing Practices regulations require careful design and scheduling. Measures other than spatial separation should be taken to further reduce the possibility of contamination. The following practices are suggested:

1. Schedule different type products for packaging operations on adjacent lines.
2. Avoid similarities in the design of packaging supplies or components on adjacent lines.

3. Prevent similar appearing products from being run at the same time on adjacent lines.
4. Schedule packaging operations sufficiently far in advance so that all contributing departments (label control, supplies, warehouse, analytical laboratory, bulk product warehouse, quality control, etc.) will be able to insure that all required procedures will be completed before packaging operations are to commence.

21 CFR 133.10(b)

[Packaging and labeling operations shall:]
(b) Provide for an inspection of the facilities prior
to use to assure that all drugs and previously used
packaging and labeling materials have been removed.

The inspection of the packaging and labeling facilities by the line supervisor prior to the start of operations consists of two complementary parts:

1. A determination that all components used for the previous operation have been removed from the partitioned area.
2. An inspection of all components, equipment, bulk product, containers, labels, labeling, and personnel to be used for the current run to insure that there is no possibility of error in the operations under his responsibility. The packaging-labeling supervisor must then document all procedures he has performed so that a record of all operations completed during packaging-labeling is made.

Cleaning procedures to be completed between packaging operations for different products or different strengths of the same drug include:

1. All loose drug and printed labels—labeling removed. Bulk materials returned to stock; drug tailings and labeling imprinted with control numbers or expiration dates destroyed.
2. All parts of packaging or filling equipment in contact with drug removed and cleaned with proper solvents.
3. Equipment not in contact with drug blown clear and wiped clean.
4. All equipment on packaging line checked for cleanliness and appropriateness by line supervisor and second knowledgeable person.

If the same strength of the same drug is being filled, packaged, and labeled under a different packaging control number:

1. All labels and labeling bearing previous control number removed and destroyed.
2. Filling hoppers cleaned of all bulk drug.
3. Line cleaned of all extraneous components from previous run.

A convenient method of standardizing and documenting control procedures is to use a form listing checks to be made by the packaging supervisor prior to operations.

Necessary data fields for such a form include:

1. Product name and number.
2. Packaging lot number used.
3. Bulk drug batch-production number.
4. Packaging line used.
5. Checks verifying that:
   a. clean equipment being used
   b. clean waste receptacles present on line
   c. no labeling from previous run present (includes stenciled, typed, or printed)
   d. no bulk or packaged drug product from previous run present; all tailings destroyed
   e. proper printed components and labels present on line
   f. proper bulk material on line—released by analytical laboratory, and expiration date not exceeded
   g. all equipment functioning properly (compressed air, lighting, labeling machines, label checkers and decoders, fill checks)
   h. packaging line identified to show product, strength, control number, bulk or packaged drug
6. Supervisor's name.
7. Date.

Data field (5a) necessitates that a clean equipment tag be present on each piece of machinery that comes in contact with the product at the start-up of each packaging-labeling operation. This can be in the form of a permanently attached card which provides a perpetual use log for the individual machine. Preferably a separate tag is attached to the equipment after cleaning, identifying the equipment and showing the date of cleaning. This tag is checked prior to each run by the supervisor and is removed and made a part of the batch record after the run.

The data field requirements of (5e) and (5f) can be satisfied by the inclusion of a specimen copy of all labels and labeling, printed components, revision numbers, stencils, and laboratory analytical releases with the packaging batch records. If the component and information requirements indicated in the packaging protocol and packaging order coincide with materials present on the line, the supervisor then signs approval for processing. Since this is a critical procedural control step, the checker-doer concept prevails and a second responsible and knowledgeable person should also endorse the documentation. This person could be the line leader for actual operation—not management-supervisory, but worker-supervisory with necessary experience.

21 CFR 133.10(c)

[Packaging and labeling operations shall:]
(c) Include the following labeling controls:

(1) The holding of labels and package labeling upon receipt pending review and proofing against an approved final copy by a competent and responsible individual to assure that they are accurate regarding identity, content, and conformity with the approved copy before release to inventory.

(2) The maintenance and storage of each type of label and package labeling representing different products, strength, dosage forms, or quantity of contents in such a manner as to prevent mixups and provide proper identification.

(3) A suitable system for assuring that only current labels and package labeling are retained and that stocks of obsolete labels and package labeling are destroyed.

(4) Restriction of access to labels and package labeling to authorized personnel.

(5) Avoidance of gang printing of cut labels, cartons, or inserts when the labels, cartons, or inserts are for different products or different strengths of the same products or are of the same size and have identical or similar format and/or color schemes. If gang printing is employed,

packaging and labeling operations shall provide
for added control procedures. These added controls should consider sheet layout, stacking, cutting, and handling during and after printing.

The requirements for label storage to avoid mixups begins with its production at either in-house or outside printing facilities. The printing operations
should be designed so that only one component or label is printed on the
same sheet. Printed components and labels must be maintained in separate
storage compartments during all phases of their manufacture. Gang printing
of more than one item per sheet is legally permissible, but the extra care
and controls required indicate it to be undesirable.

Control of labels also requires that:

1. No foreign labels or labeling in the vicinity of printing, cutting, rolling,
   folding, assembling, glueing operations.
2. No missing print—frequent samples withdrawn to insure proper print.
3. No splicing on roll labels.
4. All containers and pallets identified; Contents taped or secured when
   operations completed.
5. Clean up following completion of job order; foreman-supervisor written
   approval prior to change-over.
6. Foreman-supervisor approval of job order prior to printing and other
   associated operations.

All printed material should arrive at the drug packaging site in individual securely wrapped containers, one job number per container, and
labeled with:

1. Contents—printed component name and number.
2. Quantity per container.
3. Total quantity in order.
4. Print order number.
5. Date.

The design of the label and labeling must be amenable to control
processes. Normally a multidigit identification code number is assigned
to each printed component. The last several numbers may be used to indicate type revisions which are made when supplemental information
changes are necessary. To insure proper label identity for the jobs, these

revisions must be carefully checked by printing quality control individually for each incoming lot. Information exchange must be timely and accurate between those organizational functions responsible for the label change to the printer, receiving printer's proofs, and examining quarantined incoming printing orders.

The permanent label record described in section 133.10(d) must list the revision numbers of all labels and labeling so that out-of-date materials may be destroyed. Acceptance and use of out-of-date labeling makes packaged contents violative.

The receiving function described previously applies also to labeling and other printed components. Accurate permanent records must be maintained of receiving, disposition, and movement of these items throughout all processing. The quarantining and isolation of all incoming lots of printed material pending approval of printing quality and the accuracy of the labeling is mandatory. Spatial separation and limited access storage should be utilized during the quarantine period.

All incoming printed material must be sampled and inspected to insure that latest revisions are being used for current operations.

Inspection of printed components includes both the content of the text and also the printing for errors and defects. Selection of low AQLs with a large number of samples permits more meaningful inference concerning the quality of the printing lot. A high incidence of defects which affect the legibility, adhesion, or the ability of machinery to handle the component should result in rejection of the lot. Defects which are minor in nature, unless present at a level greater than 5%, should not result in rejection. These rejects include:

1. Dirty, scuffed, or small tears not on printed legend.
2. Folds.
3. Excess glue.

Records and samples of each job order must be maintained as a permanent quality control record. Material not meeting specifications is rejected and isolated pending a disposition decision of return or destruction. The decision must be stated on the record as well as the person making the decision and the person taking action on the decision.

Approved material is released to the label issuance area for controlled distribution to specific packaging operations. A label room supervisor has the responsibility for the label stock turned over to him from receiving.

Separate cubicles or other adequate physical separation for each label type should be plentiful. This will allow near-alikes to be kept far apart. The same should be done for labeling, that is, package inserts or brochures or product cards that may be combined with the drug in the final package.

The labeling supervisor should accept responsibility for final label review and each time a particular run uses a particular label (and labeling), he should certify to its conformity with the labeling specified in the batch production records. This should be certified in the label issue record described in 133.10(d).

Revisions in the content of labels, labeling, and printed components may be made as a result of regulatory decisions or company policy. Approved changes to content may be indicated on the copy by either altering the code number of the packaging component each time a revision is made or by adding a consecutively numbered prefix or suffix to the code number. If revision numbers are included on printed components, it is necessary to insure the correctness of the label-labeling being used in finishing operations immediately before operations commence. For this reason, a current copy of latest printing revisions should be retained in an area immediately accessible to packaging operations. A responsible and competent employee must verify their correctness, and sign and date the component's release on the permanent batch records maintained for packaging and labeling operations.

To insure proper label printing and identity, any revision in content must also be carefully checked by printing quality control and by the label inspection function for each incoming lot. Information exchanges between those organizational elements responsible for label changes to the printer, printing quality control, label inspection, and label issue must be timely and accurate. The permanent label record (section 133.10(d)) must list the revision numbers for all printed components so that out-of-date material may be collected and destroyed.

21 CFR 133.10(d)

[Packaging and labeling operations shall:]
(d) Provide strict control of the package labeling issued for use with the drug. Such issue shall be carefully checked by a competent and responsible person for identity and conformity to the labeling specified in the batch production record. Said record shall identify the labeling and the quantities issued and used and shall reasonably reconcile any

discrepancy between the quantity of drug finished
and the quantities of labeling issued. All excess
package labeling bearing lot or control numbers
shall be destroyed. In event of any significant unexplained discrepancy, an investigation should be
carried out according to § 133.8(h).

Control of label issuance extends beyond the quantity to include also when,
how, and to whom labels are released.

Quantity

The label issue supervisor should be advised prior to labeling operations of
the exact quantity of labels and labeling required for each packaging run.
This allows the preparation of a suitable number of counted labels in time
for operations. Only limited amounts of labels should be issued at any one
time. If a large run requiring more than two rolls of labels is scheduled, return trips to the label issue office is a more controlled practice than releasing
excess labels which might be lost or misplaced. Aside from this exception,
the amount of labels and labeling issued should correspond to the amount of
the packaging order. A small overage is permissible to allow for those labels
which will be damaged, poorly printed or used for setting up.

Method

Accountability of all labels is insured through the maintenance of (1) the
permanent label record, a perpetual inventory of all acceptable labels released
to label issuance by label inspection; and (2) the label issue record, which
logs all labels as they are transferred to packaging and labeling. The two
may be combined so long as the following data fields are permanently
maintained.

1. Quantity and identification of each printing order of labels received.
2. Disposition of all labels received by the packaging control number to
   which they are issued.
3. Person issuing labels—signature and date.
4. Person receiving labels—signature and date.
5. Quantity of labels returned, including damaged labels.
6. Certification of return of labels and label roll cores by person returning and
   person receiving—date of return.

7. Destruction of excess labels printed with control numbers is certified and dated.
8. Reconciliation and justification of all labels issued.

Labels should be issued in sealed containers, (plastic bags are suitable) after counting. Only one label or labeling type should be handled at one time to prevent mixup.

When—to Whom

Labels should only be issued to a packaging line after the line supervisor certifies that the line to be utilized is free from labels and labeling from previous operations. A label issue account form certifying to this fact should be presented to the label issue function at the time these printed components are received by the designated individual (packaging line leader). This label issue account can also serve as a tally for label accountability computations at the conclusion of the run. After completion, it is included with the batch packaging protocol. Pertinent data fields include:

1. Area cleanliness certified by supervisor of [line, date].
2. Labels and labeling received by [   ].
3. Quantity issued (matching requirements of the packaging order).
4. Code number and name of labels issued (matching requirements of the packaging protocol).
5. Quantity returned intact.
6. Quantity returned damaged.
7. Quantity destroyed.
8. Quantity on rejected material.
9. Total of (5) through (8) above.
10. Quantity of (9) minus quantity of (3).
11. Quantity packaged.
12. Loss or gain.
13. Justification for (12).
14. Line supervisor at completion—date.
15. Label supervisor at completion—date.

This completed form becomes a part of the permanent batch packaging record.

21 CFR 133.10(e)

[Packaging and labeling operations shall:]
(e) Provide for adequate examination or laboratory testing of [adequately] representative samples of finished products after packaging and labeling to safeguard against any errors in the finishing operations, and to prevent distribution of any batch until all specified tests have been met.

Compliance with the intent of this subsection requires that the inspection process continue throughout the labeling-packaging operations to prevent incorrect components or procedures from being utilized. Since it is most economical to make the examination of finished products at the time of packaging and labeling, that procedure normally is followed. Inspection at this time also permits immediate feedback to the manufacturing functions so that corrections may be made with no further output of defective material.

An inspection force to make periodic audits of the work line, printed components used in market packages, and finally the product itself must be established for these operations. Quality control normally functions in the capacity of an independent check on the correctness of production operations. As with manufacturing audits and inspections, although quality cannot be inspected into a product, operating confidence levels of quality may be statistically determined by these examinations and deviant material prevented from leaving the plant. Samples are drawn as a function of the number of finished units in the lot and appropriate acceptable quality levels determined for different classes of possible defects. Quality control must have the power to segregate suspected defective lots of packaged materials and be free of pressure from the production or marketing functions of the organization.

Product leaving the packaging, labeling, and final inspection operations must be placed in a quarantine area to prevent market distribution until final quality control approval for release is obtained. Each group of containers holding market packages must be appropriately and conspicuously tagged to prevent inadvertent use while in quarantine.

Final quality control release must be preceded by the satisfactory completion of the following events:

1. Quality control laboratory release of the product as meeting manufacturing and packaging specificaitons.

2. Retention by the quality control laboratory of sufficient finished market containers for stability testing and for retained samples for future testing.
3. Quality control audit of packaging-labeling operation is within acceptable quality level tolerances.
4. Label-labeling accountability between amount issued and amount utilized or returned/destroyed is acceptable.
5. Finished goods warehouse accountability of received quarantined market packages with amount packaged and labeled is acceptable.

The coordination of these information inputs should be the responsibility of the quality control department. Cards listing the requirements for each of the inputs should be submitted by the concerned department to quality control stating:

1. Product name and number.
2. Packaging control number.
3. Acceptable laboratory results or acceptable accountability results with specific amounts.
4. Signature of responsible authority.
5. Date.

These cards become a part of the permanent batch packaging records after being processed by quality control. Quality control should also maintain a permanent record of its handling of final releases.

Once release has been given to a packaging control number, quarantine tags on the containers should be removed by a quality control representative and release labeling applied. Quality control must have the sole authority to remove these quarantine notices, permitting shipment of the lot.

Additional Packaging and Labeling Control Measures

Going beyond packaging needs, all best efforts in preparing a tidy and proper product can be frustrated by inadequate shipment packaging, incompetent or or unconscientious carriers, and failures in warning for storage needs on the outer carton.

The element of security plays a substantial role here, and many manufacturers are to be commended for their appreciation of that fact. While this is especially true of shipments of narcotics, exempt narcotics, barbiturates, amphetamines, and any dangerous or abusable drugs, the same principles attach to all prescription drugs and investigational drugs. The payoff for "filchers" of drugs is so disproportionate to the penalties that organized crime has moved into this area. The man who steals auto tires from a shipment does well if he gets half the legitimate price of the stolen tire. The man who steals drugs, in many instances will get 10 or 20 times its list value on the illicit drug market.

Security measures at the manufacturing and shipping installations and a system of cartonization and carrier control is a necessary part of the drug distribution system.

Chapter 11

LABORATORY CONTROLS

21 CFR 133.11   Laboratory controls.

Laboratory controls shall include the establishment
of scientifically sound and appropriate specifications, standards, and test procedures to assure that
components, in-processed drugs, and finished
products conform to appropriate standards of
identity, strength, quality, and purity.

Quality control laboratories normally consist of two units—an analytical laboratory, and a microbiological laboratory. The former performs chemical
assays and tests on incoming raw materials and components, work in
process, and finished goods, to insure compliance to official drug compendia
and/or in-house specifications. The microbiology unit performs a variety of
tests including those for microbiological contamination in incoming raw
materials and in specified components. Plate counts taken during sterile operations are incubated and monitored. The appropriate sterility testing is
completed on all ointments, parenterals, and ophthalmics prior to release for
distribution. Frequently, the quality control laboratories may have a research
function to develop more accurate, economical and precise analytical methods.
    Specifications and test procedures are, in many instances, dictated by
official compendia, the United States Pharmacopeia, or the National
Formulary. Although established compendial procedures are the final arbiters,
the pharmaceutical manufacturer is allowed to substitute other procedures or

automated equipment into analytical sequences as long as the results are comparable to those obtained using the official protocols.

In-house testing methods for nonofficial drugs or components must consistently yield uniform results so as to insure the safety and efficacy of the final product. The development of these requirements is a joint function of research and development, product specifications, and quality control laboratories.

Separate records must be maintained for raw materials, work-in-process, and final market packages by the laboratory, so that the identity, purity, strength, and quality of the drug may be demonstrated during all stages of its production.

21 CFR 133.11(a)

[Laboratory controls shall include:]
(a) The establishment of master records containing appropriate specifications for the acceptance of each lot of drug components, product containers, and their components used in drug production and packaging and a description of the sampling and testing procedures used for them. Said samples shall be representative and adequately identified. Such records shall also provide for appropriate retesting of drug components, product containers, and their components subject to deterioration.

The analytical laboratory must develop testing specifications for each component and raw material utilized in the drug product and its production. As mentioned in the section on assigned numerical systems, these items are ordered by an item number and name, and, when received at the plant, are assigned a sequential control number which is used to control their use and accountability. The received material assigned to any single control number is output from one cycle of a manufacturer's production and should represent a homogeneous unit.

The requirements of this subsection, then, include the development of analytical and testing procedures and target values and tolerances for each item arriving at the plant. A representative sample from each assigned control number must meet the requirements of its protocol before the material may be used.

The testing specifications established for each item includes the following data fields:

1. Product name and number.
2. Required tests—this can refer to compendial requirements or in-house specifications, but should include:
   a. amount of sample necessary for testing and retention for future analyses
   b. amount of each reagent, buffer, etc. necessary for tests
   c. equipment necessary for tests
   d. instrumentation required for tests
   e. personnel qualifications required for each test
   f. exact sequencing and testing procedures written in detail
   g. sample equations for computations
3. A target value and tolerances allowable for each test. This should reflect compendial requirements or similarly stringent in-house variance limits. For official drugs, in-house tolerances should be less than compendial values to insure that all released product meets official requirements when subjected to regulatory inspection and testing.
4. The frequency for reassaying each item. A maximum of one year for stable (loss of potency less than 3% per year) components and raw materials is recommended.

Also required is the establishment of a sampling protocol for obtaining components and raw materials samples. It should include the following data fields:

1. Who has the authority to sample received goods?
2. Quantity to be sampled based on the number of incoming containers per control number.
3. Method of selecting containers to be sampled.
4. Size and distribution of sample from each container.
5. Instructions for packaging and labeling the sample container.
6. Labeling and resealing instructions for the sampled container(s).
7. Entering sample information in the continuous log maintained in the control laboratory.

The testing specifications and sampling protocol are official master records and must be maintained in a secure locked storage area with limited access. The master records should be placed under the control of a single, competent person with appropriate academic training and experience to make necessary and appropriate corrections, additions or deletions. The documentation requirements for packaging components found in 21 CFR 133.9 are identical with those for chemical components.

21 CFR 133.11(b)

[Laboratory controls shall include:]
(b) A reserve sample of all active ingredients as
required by § 133.6(h).

As required by section 133.6(h), the reserve sample for each pharmacologically active ingredient in the product is not less than twice the quantity required for all tests except those for sterility and presence of pyrogens. The reserve sample must be kept for two years after completion of distribution of the last drug lot incorporating it or one year after the last expiration date, whichever is longer.

A prudent manufacturer will retain a reserve sample of all raw materials and packaging components as well as in-process samples equal to several times the amount required for all testing in order to determine the validity of any complaints about the product.

This reserve is in addition to samples retained for stability testing.

21 CFR 133.11(c), (d)

[Laboratory controls shall include:]
(c) The establishment of master records, when
needed, containing specifications and a description
of sampling and testing procedures for in-process
drug preparations. Such samples shall be adequately
representative and properly identified.

(d) The establishment of master records containing a description of sampling procedures and appropriate specifications for finished drug products.
Such samples shall be adequately representative
and properly identified.

Specifications for work-in-process and finished products must meet the same stringent requirements imposed on raw materials. Dosage form samples must be assayed to insure that the purity, identity, and potency is as claimed and that the quality and elegance of the product is as desired. Specifications define the physical and chemical parameters for the formulation.

Compendial monographs for sterility, dissolution, weight variation, and content uniformity are quite specific, as are assay methods for official drugs. Achieving compliance to compendial requirements is considered as meeting minimal quality criteria. The product manufacturer pursues the spirit rather than the letter of the law and develops additional, more specific, and more stringent tests to insure the quality of his product, even though he may not label it as "exceeding compendial requirements." Most formulation and in-process controls are not included in the compendia and therefore must be developed. Specification design must be carried out by juxtaposing what the firm desires as an ideal in its product against cost factors, official standards, those standards submitted with the New Drug Application, and the limitations of the laboratory. The specifications for each product should be developed and recorded as an official document and include the following data fields:

1. Product name and number.
2. Required tests—referencing to compendial and official requirements if applicable, or in-house specifications. These might include:
   a. potency tests
   b. identity tests of ingredients, known contaminants and degradation products
   c. hardness, friability, viscosity
   d. dimension
   e. color determination
   f. moisture determination
   g. pH determination
   h. oxygen determination
   i. weight variation or content uniformity
   j. disintegration or dissolution time
   k. visual defects (chipping, mottling, coating defects)
   l. abrasiveness or foreign material present in ointments or ophthalmic products
   m. sterility
3. Amount of drug, buffer, reagent required for each test.
4. Equipment requirements for each test.
5. Personnel requirements for each task; job level, training, experience.
6. Exact test or assay performance description.
7. Sample equations.

8. Allowable tolerances or variance for each test.
9. Submission or recording of required data.
10. Basis for sampling.

Each batch of manufactured material might be considered to be homogeneous if the processing steps have been carefully designed and controlled since the materials entering the production sequence are uniform and processed identically. The laboratory tests for product approval should be performed at the batch level rather than for the entire lot in order to prevent leveling of variance and distortion of test results. Since batch uniformity cannot be extrapolated to subsequent production output, testing should be performed on samples which manufacturing withdraws at regular intervals during processing. A statistically significant representative quantity of these control samples should be randomly selected and subjected to analytical procedures as the basis for release of each batch.

Samples from each batch should be submitted to the quality control laboratory in sealed containers labeled to show:

1. Product name and number.
2. Lot and batch number.
3. Last manufacturing operation completed.
4. Time and date of run.
5. Operator and supervisor.

Manufacturing protocols should be devised so that the movement of in-process product depends upon the satisfactory completion of the testing required at each stage. This is economical since it prevents subsequent processing of defective material and the marketing of violative finished goods.

21 CFR 133.11(3) (1), (2), (3), (4)

[Laboratory controls shall include:]
(e) Adequate provisions for checking the identity and strength of drug products for all active ingredients and for assuring:

(1) Sterility of drugs purported to be sterile and freedom from objectionable micro-organisms for those drugs which should be so by virtue of their intended use.

(2) The absence of pyrogens for those drugs purporting to be pyrogen-free.

(3) Minimal contamination of ophthalmic ointments by foreign particles and harsh or abrasive
substances.

(4) That the drug release pattern of sustained release products is tested by laboratory methods to
assure conformance to the release specifications.

Specific testing required for inclusion in master product formulae are delineated
in this section. Administratively, the operating policies of the quality control
laboratories must insure that these requirements necessary for measuring
product purity, identity, quality and strength, are satisfactorily completed before the drug is released for marketing. Quality assurance of marketed products
is maximized when specific and accurate testing methods are included in
product specifications for each dosage form.

Methods for testing the identity, purity, and strength of each active ingredient must be specific for the drug substance, excluding interference from
any reactant, contaminant or degradation product. Contaminants include solvents, inorganic impurities, heavy metals, byproducts, isomer forms, and
excipients found in the dosage form.

Testing procedures described in subsections (1), (2), and (3) must be
performed after finishing operations, since filling procedures and the product
container may both serve as contamination sources. Compendia describe minimal testing procedures to determine conformance. Good Manufacturing
Practices compliance requires that the sampling procedures are adequate enough
to provide a representative picture of the batch. For terminally sterilized
products, samples must be withdrawn from different locations in the sterilizing
unit and also for each unit utilized. Each sample should then be tested. Biological indicators and challenge microorganisms are gaining acceptance as an
additional method for achieving assurance of product quality for the
manufacturer.

This method is highly recommended since the best proof that a lot of
material subjected to sterilization procedures has a high probability of being
sterile, is the destruction of calibrated doses of resistant organisms of defined resistance [1]

Other dosage units must have a sufficient number of representative
samples taken throughout the finishing cycle for test purposes.

Sustained release dosage form profiles must be established during the
research and development phase in vivo. Biopharmaceutical in vitro models
may then be developed for analytical testing by utilizing a variety of
techniques. It is essential that the areas under the curves be equivalent to

those developed for the in vivo condition. Again, the sampling of finished dosage forms for analysis must provide units representative of the lot.

21 CFR 133.11(f)

[Laboratory controls shall include:]
(f) Adequate provision for auditing the reliability, accuracy, precision, and performance
of laboratory test procedures and laboratory instruments used.

This subsection infers that adequate control measures will be utilized within the laboratory to monitor the accuracy and precision of analytical techniques employed. The reliability of the testing sequence may be established by em-ploying several methods concurrently, by determining recoveries using standard addition methods, or by assay of carefully prepared materials with known values. Enough replicate tests should be performed to determine not only average recovery but also a reliable standard deviation and a measure of the sensitivity of the assay.

Initially, the only personnel performing each test procedure should be those that are properly qualified by education, training, and experience. Thus personnel accountability is the first check. So that this accountability may be documented, personnel records should be maintained for each laboratory employee. This includes:

1. Name.
2. Academic training and degrees—dates.
3. Relevant experience: place, description, dates.
4. Refresher courses—training: subject, place, dates.
5. Publications—dates.
6. Honors—recognition.
7. Responsibilities in the laboratory and list of assays the person is qualified to perform.

Even the most qualified personnel cannot perform tests properly unless instrumentation and equipment are available and properly maintained. Rec-ords of all maintenance and calibration for each piece of laboratory equipment must be kept. Such equipment and records would include:

1. Balances: A permanent record log should be kept, with one balance to a page, listing:

  a. manufacturer
  b. date of purchase
  c. type
  d. serial number
  e. capacity
  f. reproducibility
  g. log of calibration and repair
    (1) date
    (2) signature of contractor
2. Colorimeters: A permanent record log should be kept, with one instrument per page, listing:
  a. manufacturer
  b. filters available
  c. log of lamp replacement and repair
3. Spectrophotometers: A permanent record log should be kept for each instrument listing:
  a. manufacturer
  b. type
  c. band-pass if of fixed band-pass type
  d. spectral range
  e. standards used for calibration
    (1) wavelength
    (2) absorbance
  f. log of calibration for wavelength and absorbance showing:
    (1) date
    (2) signature of operator
    (3) deviations found
  g. log of lamp replacement
  h. repair log
    (1) date
    (2) signature of contractor
4. pH meters: A separate record should be kept for each instrument listing:
  a. manufacturer
  b. reproducibility
  c. log of electrode replacement showing
    (1) electrode type
    (2) date of replacement
    (3) reason for replacement
5. Instruments used for moisture determination.
  a. drying ovens with thermometer

b. vacuum ovens with thermometer and vacuum gauge
c. "moisture balance"
d. Karl Fisher dead-stop titrator
6. Volumetric glassware.
   a. all volumetric ware should be marked "Class A" or "NBS certified," or be of known tolerance
   b. sufficient quantities of common sizes should be available in:
      (1) pipets
      (2) burets
      (3) volumetric flasks
      (4) cylinders
      (5) graduated test tubes
7. Additional instruments.
Other laboratory instruments such as
   a. refractometer
   b. melting point apparatus
   c. polarimeter
   d. X-ray diffraction equipment
   e. gas chromatograph
   f. infrared spectrophotometer
   g. atomic absorption spectrometer should each have a separate entry recording:
      (1) manufacturer
      (2) log of calibration
      (3) log of repair

Since most instrumental methods require reference substances to standardize quantitative and qualitative determinations, standard materials should be logged under the following headings:

1. International standard.
2. USP reference.
3. NF reference.
4. House standard.

The house standard should be labeled as to purity. Each log should contain:

1. Name
2. Date of manufacture.

3. Date opened.
4. Expiration date.

Standard solutions for volumetric analysis require rigid control.

1. Each solution properly labeled:
   a. name
   b. nominal strength
   c. volumetric factor
   d. date of preparation
2. Each solution properly prepared:
   a. name of commercial supplier
   b. name of supplier of standard concentrate
   c. log of each solution prepared in the laboratory showing:
      (1) formula for preparation
      (2) directions for standardization
      (3) standardization by analysis in triplicate
      (4) periodic restandardization
      (5) signature of person preparing solution
      (6) date of preparation
      (7) signatures of people standardizing or restandardizing
3. Standard buffers: At least two standard buffers are required for the calibration of pH meters. Each container of buffer should show:
   a. nominal value of buffer to two decimal places
   b. table of change of pH with temperature
   c. date bottle was opened (USP requires fresh buffer every three months)

Finally, internal quality control procedures must facilitate correct operations. The use of control charts to record the analysis results for consecutive batches of a single product provides a means of detecting nonrandom variation and undesirable trends either in production or in the laboratory. The submission of previously analyzed samples and standard samples to periodically check the accuracy of analytical procedures and quality control personnel may also be employed. For continuous automated analysis, standard should be assayed at regular intervals to correct for drift and to assure the accuracy of the results.

21 CFR 133.11(g)

[Laboratory controls shall include:]
(g) A properly identified reserve sample of the

finished product (stored in the same immediate container-closure system in which the drug is marketed) consisting of at least twice the quantity necessary to perform all the required tests, except those for sterility and determination of the absence of pyrogens, and stored under conditions consistent with product labeling shall be retained for at least 2 years after the drug distribution has been completed or at least 1 year after the drug's expiration date, whichever is longer.

The samples to be held in retention during the shelf life of the drug should be removed at the time of the packaging-labeling operations. Samples should be taken for every lot of packaged finished goods, even though the same lot of bulk drug product may be used in more than one packaging lot. The label on the retained sample should indicate the production lot number of the drug for cross reference purposes.

The number of samples to be retained should be included in the packaging protocol so that laboratory or quality control personnel taking samples have adequate guidelines. The packaging protocol must be completed as samples are removed to show:

1. Number of samples removed.
2. Person removing samples.
3. Time and date of sampling.

All samples must be stored under conditions which simulate marketing conditions as indicated on the labeling, preferably in custody of the control laboratory.

The quantity of sample specified is a minimum. Regulatory testing and resolution of customer complaints may require more. A prudent manufacturer will, therefore, retain a larger sample than specified.

21 CFR 133.11(h)

[Laboratory controls shall include:]
(h) Provision for retaining complete records [laboratory tests performed, including the dates and endorsements of individuals making the tests, with provision for specifically relating the tests to each batch of drug] of all laboratory data relating to

each batch or lot of drug to which they apply.
Such records shall be retained for at least 2 years
after distribution has been completed or 1 year
after the drug's expiration date, whichever is
longer.

The laboratory analytical procedure least likely to result in error would be to duplicate and follow the master specifications for raw materials, work-in-process, and finished goods. The master copy, with test results, supervisory endorsements, instrument recording charts, computations and other necessary analytical data, would then be retained as a permanent record either in the laboratory or accompanying the batch records into archives.

If this method is not employed by the quality control laboratory, analytical release for each of the stages of production must be specifically referenced to the exact sequences which tested the acceptability for the material. This information is retained in the laboratory notebooks, a log of all work performed within the laboratory. Each notebook:

1. Shall be kept in permanent, bound form, with consecutively numbered pages.
2. Shall contain all data, all assay, and test results.
3. Shall indicate discarded data by drawing a single light line through the entry. It should still be legible through the line. An explanation for the correction should be entered.
4. Records of tests should include:
   a. name and lot, stock or batch number of sample
   b. name of individual who obtained sample
   c. all methods of analysis (may be by reference to official or standard methods)
   d. all raw data (such as weights, buret readings, volumes, dilutions) properly identified by reference to test procedure and labeled with units of measurement
   e. calculations, with units of measurement shown, including a sample calculation with explanation if calculation is involved or unusual
   f. statement of permitted tolerances and limits
   g. statement of compliance or noncompliance with specification
   h. date and signature of person performing test and of person checking the calculations. An independent computation by the checker should be shown
   i. signed and dated statement by the laboratory supervisor of approval or rejection of material, and recommendation for disposal

The laboratory should maintain a permanent sequential record of all material checked into the department, indexed by the numerical code assigned to it. These logs should be readily available and indicate the status of the material, dates of processing, and whether necessary analytical testing has been satisfactorily completed. Rework material resubmitted following further processing should also be indicated along with its fate.

Inherent in the operation of the quality control laboratory and any quality control audit or inspection system is the capacity and authority to quarantine any product or component at any stage in processing. To prevent the adulteration and misbranding of drugs, a necessary function is restricting the acceptance, further production, or release of product only to those materials possessing desired attributes as defined in specifications. The following guidelines are applicable to materials rejected for any reason during the production sequence:

1. The entire batch or lot is isolated immediately in restricted quarantine area.
2. Each container of the quarantined lot is labeled to indicate its status. Label indicates a number which cross-references records for history and explanation of rejection action.
3. Appropriate departments notified of rejection:
   a. raw materials: purchasing department and warehouse
   b. work-in-process: manufacturing manager
   c. finished goods: finished goods warehouse
4. All pertinent information listed in central data file maintained by quality control.

Rejection Log

The quality control function must have the sole authority to control the movement of rejected material. It must, therefore, maintain information files concerning the amounts of rejected materials and their disposition. The rejection log acts as the central information center for this data. The log contains:

1. Rejection number assigned to material. These generally follow a sequential system with one rejection number for each new lot or batch found to be defective.
2. Name and product or item number of rejected material.
3. Date rejection made.
4. Source of rejected material (vendor, department in which manufactured or discovered).

5. Person entering rejection and responsible for conducting investigation to ascertain cause.
6. Reason for rejection or reference to control laboratory data.
7. Satisfactory method for removing quarantine (return to vendor, discard, rework).
8. Date of quarantine removal with authorizing signature.

Unless a complete investigation of the causes for each rejection is conducted, this procedure has only minimal value. Feedback information supplied to the manufacturing department responsible for the reject provides a means of error identification. Permanant deviations from procedures delineated in the master formula to correct the error source must first be approved by regulatory agencies for items produced under an approved NDA.

21 CFR 133.11(i)

[Laboratory controls shall include:]
(i) Provision that animals shall be maintained and controlled in a manner that assures suitability for their intended use. They shall be identified and appropriate records maintained to determine the history of use.

Minimum standards for the care and health of research and test animals are described in references [2] and [3]. In addition to these requirements, current interpretation of Good Manufacturing Practices would regard animals as sources of product contamination. Considerations such as separate facilities, constructed away from manufacturing areas, with closed water, waste removal, air conditioning and other systems would, therefore, be ideal. If these are not possible due to construction or other limitations, animal areas should be segregated as far as possible from all production activities with closed air, water and waste systems as well as limited personnel access. The same standards of cleanliness prescribed for other work areas are also applicable to these spaces.

Record requirements for animals are necessary to maintain control of their use in experimentation, testing or assay procedures. Data fields for individual animals should include:

1. Identification number or letter assigned to each animal or group of animals.
2. Characteristics and description of animal.
3. Source of animals (breeder, vendor).

4. Date of arrival.
5. Age at arrival.
6. How used.
7. Date used.

If the animal is to be used for repeated assay procedures (e.g., pyrogen testing) a time period sufficient to permit complete clearance of the drug and recovery of the test animal is required.

21 CFR 133.11(j)

[Laboratory controls shall include:]
(j) Provision that firms which manufacture non-penicillin products (including certifiable antibiotic products) on the same premises or use the same equipment as that used for manufacturing penicillin products, or that operate under any circumstances that may reasonably be regarded as conducive to contamination of other drugs by penicillin, shall test such nonpenicillin products to determine whether any have become cross-contaminated by penicillin. Such products shall not be marketed if intended for use in man [orally or parenterally] and the product is contaminated with an amount of penicillin equivalent to 0.05 unit or more of penicillin G per maximum single dose recommended in the labeling.

This appears to be an interim regulation permitting low-level contamination of drug products with penicillin. It is expected that in time the permitted tolerance will be at the "undetectable" level. If there were proper control of all sources of cross-contamination, there would be no need for this testing.

NOTES

1. C. W. Bruch, *Australas J. Pharm. Sci.,* **NS 2**, 1-8 (1973).

2. Dept. of Agriculture *Federal Register,* **32**, 3270-82, 1967.

3. *Guide for Laboratory Animal Facilities and Care* (U.S. PHS Pub. 1024), Washington, D.C., 1968.

Chapter 12

DISTRIBUTION RECORDS

21 CFR 133.12   Distribution records

(a) Finished goods warehouse control and distribution procedures shall include a system by which the distribution of each lot of drug can be readily determined to facilitate its recall if necessary. Records within the system shall contain the name and address of the consignee, date and quantity shipped, and lot or control number of the drug. Records shall be retained for at least 2 years after the distribution of the drug has been completed or 1 year after the expiration date of the drug, whichever is longer.

(b) To assure the quality of the product, finished goods warehouse control shall also include a system whereby the oldest approved stock is distributed first whenever possible. (See 21 CFR 1304 for regulations relating to manufacturing and distribution records of drugs subject to the Drug Abuse Control Amendments of 1965; Public Law 89-74).

Distribution records must be constructed and procedures established to facilitate recall of defective product. A requisite of the system is approval and specific release of each lot of drug by the quality control function before distribution can occur. This control of finished goods for shipment allows into commerce only those drugs which have been shown by testing to be nonviolative.

The manufacturer must maintain records of all distribution transactions involving in-process or finished goods. All records should be sub-indexed either by the manufacturing batch/lot number or the packaging control number as a means of accountability until the shipment passes from the direct control of the manufacturer. This type of indexing permits an efficient determination of the receiver of a recallable lot since only one shipment record need be examined. Depending on the marketing procedures of the individual company, distribution records may list shipments to consignees for packaging or labeling, or to an independent distributor, a wholesaler, a retail pharmacist, a physician, or possibly the ultimate consumer.

Total quality control of drugs requires that adequate precautionary measures shall be taken to maintain the safety and efficacy of the product. If special storage conditions have been utilized at the site of manufacturing and processing, these conditions should be continued during the distribution process. The requirement should be conspicuously labeled on each shipping container. These precautions should be documented on the order and bill of lading and maintained in the records of the shipping transaction kept by the manufacturer.

Relevant data fields for distribution records include:

1. Order number and date.
2. Name and number of each product shipped.
3. Quantity of each product shipped.
4. Lot, batch and/or packaging control number of each product.
5. Consignee's order number.
6. Consignee's name, address, and applicable registration numbers.
7. Method of distribution or shipment.
8. Name of distributor—address.
9. Date of shipment.
10. Special precautions utilized.

Although a variety of distribution recording systems may be utilized, the Food and Drug Administration considers it important that the lot or control number be placed on retained copies of shipping invoices as a minimum precaution.

The distribution process also includes other considerations. It must be arranged so that a first in-first out movement of product occurs. This requirement is consistent with the intent of the stability and expiration dating policy. The distribution system must include provisions so that this movement is achieved.

All distribution records must be maintained for a minimum two-year period after the distribution process for any control number has been completed. If expiration dating longer than two years is used for a product, distribution records should be maintained at least for one year past the expected life of the product. Attention is drawn to the wording of this section, which indicates a two-year minimum period for record retention, but also seems to imply a longer period if necessary to facilitate recall if the particular item remains in commerce for a period longer than two years.

Chapter 13

STABILITY

21 CFR 133.13   Stability

There shall be assurance of the stability of finished
drug products.

The determination of stability characteristics of the finished dosage form over
extended time periods projects the concept of total quality control to the
consumer. Laboratory analysis, manufacturing techniques, and quality control procedures prior to market release attempt to insure product purity,
identity, strength, and quality at the completion of the manufacturing
processes. Stability studies demonstrate that the necessary critical characteristics present at the time of production and release can be expected to be
present when the dosage form is administered. If safety and efficacy values
decline, stability studies provide information to determine when and under
what conditions the product should be withdrawn from the market.
   Effective stability studies must include provisions of:

1. Specific chemical and physical characteristics desired at time of
   administration.
2. Analytical procedures and tests to determine the degree to which these
   characteristics are present.
3. Allowable tolerances and variation for each critical characteristic.
4. Anticipated shelf-life under the mot severe anticipated environment before product characteristics are out of specifications.

5. Recommended physical, chemical, and environmental conditions for holding the drug product during preadministration storage.

Considerations for these requirements must occur early in the research and development phase. Physical and chemical parameters dictate many of the characteristics that will be inherent in the dosage form. Some important considerations are:

1. The crystal form of drug substance when polymorphs have different bioavailability and stability.
2. Solubility and stability characteristics in various solvents.
3. Acid-base dissociation constants influencing selection of optimum pH levels.
4. pH values necessary for greatest stability affecting the choice of buffers, chelating agents and antioxidant used in formulation.
5. Hardness, friability, dissolution, and disintegration times are determined by particle size, solubility, rate of solution, aggregation, and wettability of the drug substance.
6. Stability under heat and light conditions affecting sterilizing methods and the container utilized.
7. The selection of the active drug moieties and excipients for the final dosage form dictates the methods of manufacture, processing, sterilization, and the container-closure to be utilized in packaging operations.

These considerations apply primarily to chemical and physical degradation determinations. In addition to these factors, testing procedures must establish significant correlation between these parameters and clinical efficacy and safety over extended time periods.

Alterations of particle size and surface area, polymorphism and physical-chemical interactions between formulation ingredients such as polymerization, hardening, induced pH changes all commonly occur. In vitro testing methods are available for monitoring these changes and extrapolating stability data.

Ultimately stability testing should insure that:

1. Degradation of the pharmaceutical preparation in its market container occurs at a consistent and predictable rate.
2. There is minimum loss of clinical effectivenss and chemical potency over a reasonable shelf life expectancy.
3. There is no transferance or migration of hazardous container components to the drug.
4. There is minimal migration of active constituents of the pharmaceutical

preparation into the container and minimal reaction with the container and closure.
5. There is minimal chemical or physical reaction between the dosage form ingredients which would jeopardize clinical effectiveness or safety.

The increasing regulatory interest in equating in vitro testing with in vivo response requires some exploration. In vitro data showing the degree of alteration of physical and chemical properties does not demonstrate the clinical manifestations of these changes. Comparative bioavailability data obtained from blood levels, excretory studies, or controlled clinical performance of "new" and "aged" lots are more meaningful indicators of change. Since this type of data is now required for New Drug Application submission to show safety and efficacy, it is not impossible that such data may be required to show stability of lots.

21 CFR 133.13(a)

[This stability shall be:
(a) Determined by reliable, meaningful and specific test methods.

Two types of stability studies must be employed in drug evaluation. The most common type of study is the storage of the drug dosage form in its market container under simulated market conditions with assay and control tests made at regular intervals. By varying temperature, humidity, and light conditions, approximations to various geographic marketing regions may be made. (See suggested readings at the end of this chapter.) The second type is the accelerated stability study. Accelerated stability studies have demonstrated that, by exaggerating environmental conditions, in many cases close approximations to actual chemical and physical degradation rates may be extrapolated.

Because of the time required to complete the first type and the numerous sources of variability introduced by testing over the entire shelf-life of the drug, it is useful to use the second type of study method as a predictive tool.

Accelerated stability studies can be designed to simultaneously test the influence of several variables and with appropriate statistical methodology determine actions and interactions between variables. The advantages of this type of testing, especially in the research and development stages, are numerous. Control variation may be established, different formulations evaluated, and analytical variability minimized.

Accelerated stability studies which have been well designed and properly performed have permitted accurate predictions of shelf-life. Kinetics and mechanisms of the degradation process as a function of pH, temperature, oxygen content, concentration, buffers, chelating and antioxidant agents, solvents, excipients, production methods and packaging components have been accurately formulated and adequately documented.

For accelerated stability testing to be effective as a predictor, however, high correlation between the results obtained from it and from long term shelf studies are necessary. Statistical comparisons of numerous accelerated studies must be made so that upper and lower limits for specific rates may be established with a high degree of confidence. These studies must then be compared with the normal shelf-life testing method data to insure that the fit between the predicted value and actual value at any given time is correct.

It should be noted that a knowledge of all the variables and their specific effects on the degradation process cannot be determined unless effective analytical procedures for intact drug and degradation products are available.

Loss of potency must be established by accurate methods capable of distinguishing the active drug from its degradation products. Degradation products must be likewise examined to insure that they have no toxic effects on the patient in the concentrations to be found in the market package. Where excipients interfere with official testing procedures, reliable alternatives must be developed and utilized.

The stability and effects of interactions of not only the active drug product, but also all elements in the formulation must be determined by studies which measure and extrapolate rates of accelerated chemical and physical changes and compare the prediction with accurate determinations of actual changes under normal conditions.

The methods for processing and presenting stability study data should present dosage acceptability as a function of time. A usual sequence is:

1. Determination of the characteristics of the drug when administered which are critical for its clinical safety and efficacy. Several parameters may be possible for any dosage type, e.g., hardness, particle size, pH, chemical potency, polymorphism, degradation.
2. Assay and testing of these characteristics at predetermined intervals so that the level of these attributes present in relation to label claims and batch analytical data taken at the time of manufacture may be made.
3. Replicate studies carried out with different pilot lots so that the actual condition of the drug may be predicted with a high degree of accuracy and confidence.

4. Utilization of linear regression techniques to compute rates of decay and alteration for each critical function under variable environmental conditions of humidity, light, and temperature.
5. Compilation of the rates of alteration and actual condition of the drug as measured by each attribute for information input to the expiration date determination.

21 CFR 133.13(b), and (c)

[This stability shall be:]
(b) Determined on products in the same container-closure system in which they are marketed.

(c) Determined on any dry drug product that is to be reconstituted at the time of dispensing (as directed in its labeling), as well as on the reconstituted product.

The intent of these two subsections is to require extensive stability testing of the drug in its marketing container and the drug as it exists following any formulation modifications that are indicated in the labeling prior to administration. Since the container may induce accelerated degradation reactions, be an additive to or an absorbant of the drug, and be ineffective in protecting the contents from environmental conditions, the selection of the container itself is made only after stringent stability tests with alternative packaging materials.

Four types of container material are commonly employed for pharmaceutical preparations: glass, plastic, rubber, and metal. Each has characteristic properties which should be recognized since they affect stability.

Glass

Glass, because of its many variations and resistance to chemical and physical change is the most commonly used container material. Several inherent limitations exist with glass:

1. Its alkaline surface may raise the pH of the pharmaceutical and induce chemical reaction.
2. Ionic radicals present in the drug may precipitate insoluble crystals from the glass.
3. The clarity of glass permits the transmission of high energy wavelengths

of light which may accelerate physical or chemical reactions in the drug.

To overcome the first two deficiencies, alternate types of commercial glass, each possessing different reactive characteristics, are available.

Boro-silicate (U.S.P. type I) glass contains fewer reactive alkali ions than the other three types of U.S.P.-recognized glass. Treatment of glass with heat and/or various chemicals as well as the use of buffers can eliminate many ionic problems normally encountered. Amber glass transmits light only at wavelengths above 470 nm, thereby reducing light-induced reactions.

Plastics

These packaging materials include a wide range of polymers of varying density and molecular weight, each possessing different physical and chemical characteristics. As a result, each must be considered in relation to the pharmaceutical which will be in contact with it to determine that no undesirable interaction occurs. Several problems are encountered with plastic:

1. Migration of the drug into the environment.
2. Transfer of environmental moisture, oxygen, and other elements into the pharmaceutical formulation.
3. Leaching of container ingredients into the drug.
4. Adsorption or absorption of the active drug or excipeints by the plastic.

Since each plastic possesses intrinsic properties, varying conditions and drug formulations must be tested to optimize stability of the final product. Again, chemical treatment of the material prior to use reduces reactivity, migration characteristics, and transmitted light. It must be remembered that neither the drug nor the container should undergo physical or chemical changes which affect the safety and efficacy of the product. The use of light transmission by plastics as a measure of light protection is complicated by the fact that plastics are only semitransparent. Light which is admitted to the container is reflected and diffused back into the product so that light energy available to degradation processes is much higher than that which might be indicated by transmission characteristics. The proper test is a diffuse reflectance measurement.

Metals

Various alloys and aluminum tubes are frequently utilized as containers for emulsions, ointments, creams, and pastes. These materials are generally inert to their contents although instances of corrosion and precipitation have been noted with products at extreme pH values or those containing metalic ions. Coating the tubes with polymers, epoxy, or other materials may reduce these tendencies, but imposes new stability problems on the pharmaceutical. The availability of new, less expensive polymers has sharply reduced the use of metal packaging components during the last few years.

Rubber

The problems of extraction of drug ingredients and leaching of container ingredients described for plastics also exist with rubber components. The use of neoprene, butyl, or natural rubber, in combination with certain epoxy, Teflon®, or varnish coatings substantially reduces drug-container interactions. The pretreatment of rubber vial stoppers and closures with water and steam removes surface blooms and also reduces potential leaching which might affect chemical analysis, toxicity, or pyrogenicity of the drug formulation.

An additional consideration which must be incorporated into the stability testing program is the way in which the product is used. For example, stability determination of a preparation in a multidose vial is inadequate unless samples are withdrawn from the container at regular intervals. Likewise, tablets in containers of 500 or 1,000 units might be adversely affected by repeated withdrawal of single or small doses. Conditions encountered during marketing must be defined and included in both accelerated and shelf-life stability testing.

21 CFR 133.13(d)

[The stability shall be:]
(d) Recorded and maintained in such manner that
the stability data may be utilized in establishing
product expiration dates.

Data derived from both accelerated and actual shelf-life stability testing of the marketed dosage form determine its expiration date. For new drugs with incomplete shelf-life studies, the expiration date should be derived from the upper confidence level of the degradation rate extrapolated from a series of accelerated studies. This results in a conservative estimate of the time interval before the product becomes unsuitable for its intended purpose.

Data must constantly be updated by the research and development function and the results communicated to the marketing and distribution sections for action. It is also necessary for management to reach a decision concerning expiration dating if the drug dosage form is so stable that decomposition over a period of years is so small that it does not affect the potency or availability of the drug. Expiration dating then may serve as a means of removing pharmaceutically unelegant drugs from distribution channels or controlling the total amount present in the market for inventory purposes.

The requirements of this section necessitate constant communications between the physical pharmacy section of research and development, who normally conduct stability studies, and the following functions:

1. Dosage form design—the objective of this liaison is the optimization of the dosage form for the finished drug product once the active ingredient has been selected.
2. NDA section—transmits stability test data for inclusion in NDA. Modifies expiration dating statement on basis of continuing studies.
3. Purchasing—transmits information concerning material specifications for chemical components, raw materials, containers, and closures based on stability studies.
4. Manufacturing and packaging—determines critical steps in manufacturing process which might adversely affect product stability (e.g., storage conditions, sterilizing procedures, time limits for in-processing).

SUGGESTED READINGS

1. J. D. Haynes, *J. Pharm. Sci.,* **60**, 927-31 (1971).
2. T. H. Riggs, *Bull. Parenteral Drug Assn.,* **25**, 116-23 (1971).

Chapter 14

EXPIRATION DATING

21 CFR 133.14   Expiration dating.

To assure that drug products liable to deterioration
meet appropriate standards of identity, strength,
quality, and purity at the time of use, the label of
all such drugs shall have suitable expiration dates
which relate to stability tests performed on the
product.

(a) Expiration dates appearing on the drug labeling
shall be justified by readily available data from stability studies such as described in § 133.13.

(b) Expiration dates shall be related to appropriate storage conditions stated on the labeling
wherever the expiration appears.

(c) When the drug is marketed in the dry state
for use in preparing a liquid product, the labeling shall bear expiration information for the
reconstituted product as well as an expiration
date for the dry product.

The function of stability testing as described in the previous section is to
provide information concerning rates of physical-chemical alteration occurring in the drug during preadministration storage. Expiration dates are determined by the use of this data to provide assurance that each administered

dose possesses the same characteristics as those which have been found to
be clinically safe and effective. Use before the expiration date insures that the
intended quality of the drug is being consumed.

Information inputs generated from stability studies define rates of alteration for key variables in the dosage formulation. These include:

1. Biological.
    a. availability, effectiveness and safety obtained from in vivo studies
    b. alterations in sterility, toxicity, pyrogens, and stability
2. Chemical.
    a. purity, identity, strength, and quality of active drug ingredients and
       antioxidants, bacteriostats, bulking, dispensing, flow, and preservative
       agents
    b. descriptions of reactions and interreactions between these agents
3. Labeling.
    a. adherence, appearance, legibility, and adequacy of labeling in relation
       to the container and the drug itself
4. Packaging container and closure.
    a. the degree to which designed characteristics of the drug are retained
       under varying environmental conditions
    b. compatability and interaction with drug and protection against
       moisture transpiration, leakage, loss of sterility, breakage by dropping
       and vibration
5. Physical.
    a. organoleptic changes in color, odor, form, clarity, and particulate
       precipitation
    b. physical alterations in viscosity, pH, surface tension, particle size,
       and compaction

Those persons determining expiration dates determine optimum levels
for each of these functions. The actual expiration date is fixed from that
critical characteristic which has the highest rate of change and attains the unacceptable level most rapidly. The product must be removed from distribution when one attribute adversely affects the clinical safety and efficacy of
the drug compound.

1. Potency drops below minimum limit.
2. There is measurable increase in toxicity or decrease in clinical effectiveness.
3. Unacceptable elements of pharmaceutical elegance appear.

4. An arbitrary date from the time of manufacture is passed, normally five years.

The final element, assignment of an arbitrary expiration date, is utilized when none of the previous three conditions indicating deterioration exist. It serves as a means for maintaining recently manufactured drug in circulation and prevents uncontrolled lengths of storage prior to administration. With no control over inventory practices of the pharmacist or physician, the manufacturer is protecting his quality standards by establishing an expiration date even when not required by evidence of deterioration during the period the product is expected to be available to the ultimate consumer.

When a company assigns expiration dates to its products it must be prepared to resupply wholesalers and retailers with replacement stocks. This necessitates coordination between marketing functions, control of returned goods, and the sales force.

Distribution centers for the dated products must be kept informed of expiration dates and insure that a first in-first out system is utilized to prevent the retention of older products. Limits must also be established so that a reasonable amount of shelf-life is available in those products sent by the manufacturer.

Chapter 15

COMPLAINT FILES

21 CFR 133.15   Complaint files.

Records shall be maintained of all written and oral
complaints regarding each product. An investigation of each complaint shall be made in accordance
with § 133.8(h). The record of each investigation
shall be maintained for at least 2 years after distribution of the drug has been completed or 1 year
after the expiration date of the drug, whichever is
longer.

Complaints received from consumers and professionals serve as the primary
means of obtaining feedback about product quality and potential sources of
danger or concern following distribution. It is necessary, therefore, that each
complaint or inquiry be evaluated by knowledgeable and responsible personnel.
      The records of production, packaging, and distribution of the drug and
the samples retained by the quality control laboratory provide the most accurate method of assessing the seriousness and the extent of the alleged deviation
which precipitated the complaint. For this reason it is also important that the
records for each production lot and packaging lot be readily available and in a
form which may be examined to solve the problem intelligently. Records
maintained by components inspection, quality control, and the laboratory
must also be available and open to the person investigating the complaint.
      Since complaints are generally received utilizing the product name and

packaging control number as the primary identifier, it is convenient to file by product and product number, with secondary filing by the packaging control number. Since this latter number is cross-referenced to the manufacturing lot and batch numbers, all records are available for inspection and evaluation, including other packaging control numbers utilizing the same manufactured batch.

Appropriate data fields for each product complaint include:

1. Serial number assigned to complaint.
2. Exact nature of complaint.
3. Name of complainant.
4. Address of complainant.
5. Date of complaint.
6. If verbal, name of person who received complaint.
7. Item name, product number, and strength.
8. Packaging control number, date of packaging.
9. Manufacturing lot and batch numbers, date.
10. Laboratory records cross-reference number, if not included with manufacturing records in archives
11. Quantity involved in complaint.
12. Size of sample obtained from complainant.
13. Evaluation of complaint.
14. Materials and records used to perform evaluation.
15. Other material possibly affected and results of its investigation
16. Signature of evaluator(s) and date.
17. Action taken by company.
18. Copy of report made to complainant.

If any such complaints involve GMP or section 501 or 502 of the Act, records must demonstrate that the complaint has either been discredited, or has engendered the changes required to preclude further complaints.

Complaints which indicate defects adversely affecting the identity, purity, potency, or quality of the drug, or defects associated with labeling, should be reported immediately to the Bureau of Compliance of the Food and Drug Administration for possible recall action. [See: P. Kahn, *Food, Drug, Cosmetic Law Journal,* **29,** 709-36 November 1972.]

Complaint files must be kept for two years after the distribution of each packaging control number has been completed or one year after the expiration date, whichever is longer. The "two years after distribution" requirement seems to be too short a period since FDA surveys have shown that some products may remain on pharmacy shelves in excess of five years. In the absence of expiration dating of all products, a prudent manufacturer should maintain the files in some form until distribution of the lot to the ultimate consumer may be expected to be completed. There may also be value to the maintenance of the file, perhaps in summary form, for the product, even after distribution of the particular lot has been completed.